Praying
the
PSALMS

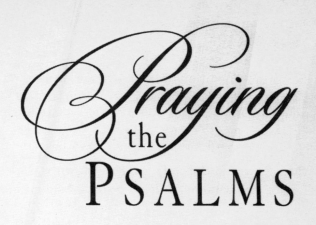

Praying the PSALMS

Clift & Kathleen
RICHARDS

Victory House, Inc.
Tulsa, Oklahoma

Praying the Psalms
Copyright © 2003 by
F. Clift and Kathleen B. Richards
ISBN 0-932081-78-9

Published by Victory House, Inc.
P.O. Box 700238
Tulsa, Oklahoma 74170
(918) 747-5009
victoryhousepublishers.com
victoryhouse.biz

Acknowledgments

The authors wish to acknowledge the capable assistance of their editor, Lloyd Hildebrand, and the staff at Victory House for their hard work, encouragement, and insightful contributions.

Contents

Psalms of Power — Prayers of Purpose

Introduction

The Book of Psalms is a rich vein of God's truth, which is waiting to be mined by every believer desiring to grow spiritually and emotionally. One way to engage in this spiritual mining process is to turn the Psalms into personal prayers that are focused on your individual needs and concerns. *Praying the Psalms* will help you to do this and to receive the spiritual treasure God has in store for you.

The men who wrote the Psalms (David, Asaph, Solomon, Moses, the sons of Korah, and others) did so under the direct guidance of the Holy Spirit (See 2 Tim. 3:16.), and they wrote in such a way that most human beings could readily identify with their feelings, aspirations, and desires.

In a very real sense, therefore, the Book of Psalms is one of the most human of all the books in the Bible. At the same time, it is a depository of spiritual truth and blessing.

The Book of Psalms is a hymnal, a personal journal, a prayer book, a devotional, a songbook, a psychological text, and a spiritual guidebook for every searching soul. Many of its passages are written in the style of personal prayers and songs that are honest and probing, as well as uplifting and faith building.

You will find that each of the Psalms readily adapts itself to your personal prayer life, and you may desire to pray one or more of the Psalms every day, as you have your quiet times with God.

The purpose of this book, therefore, is to lead you into the empowering and life-changing realm of praying the Psalms, which represent almost every hope, fear, dream, and struggle of the human soul and spirit.

If you've ever found it difficult to pray about your worries, sorrows, fears, and regrets, let the Psalms help you, for in them you will find the expression of every human emotion, from sadness and depression to joy and exultation. The prayers in this book are arranged in such a way as to help you find the topics and needs you will want to address in your personal prayer life.

As you personalize and pray the Psalms, the One who created your spirit, soul, and body will speak to your heart and help you find your way to the place of peace, protection, and power described by David: "One thing I have desired of the Lord, that will I seek: that I may dwell in the house of the Lord all the days of my life, to behold the beauty of the Lord, and to inquire in His temple.

"For in the time of trouble He shall hide me in His pavilion; in the secret place of His tabernacle He shall hide me; He shall set me high upon a rock" (Ps. 27:4-5, NKJV).

No matter what his circumstances were, David always went to God, and the Psalms he wrote show how he did so and how you may do so as well. God knows your heart, and He knows every need of your spirit, soul, and body.

Never forget that He has promised to meet those needs. Paul writes, "And my God shall supply all your need according to His riches in glory by Christ Jesus" (Phil. 4:19, NKJV).

This clarion truth is an echo of the words of David: "The Lord is my shepherd; I shall not want" (Ps. 23:1, NKJV). These are promises for you to claim in prayer.

As a youth, David served as a shepherd. He knew how much sheep need a shepherd's care, guidance, protection, and provision. Therefore, it was perfectly natural for him to use this poignant and beautiful metaphor comparing God's people to sheep and the Lord God to a shepherd.

The Psalms reveal how God, as your glorious Shepherd, is willing and able to take care of you, as you go through life. Therefore, it is both logical and responsible to pray the Psalms, for, by doing so, you will find that they are powerful antidotes to any fear, despair, discouragement, confusion, and depression you may encounter along the way. In the process, your faith will be strengthened, your heart will be lifted, and your soul will be restored.

Start this exciting journey by personalizing and praying Psalm 23, the best known of all the Psalms. Make it your personal prayer, an expression of faith and a hymn of praise to your Shepherd, who is also your heavenly Father.

Known as the Shepherd's Psalm, Psalm 23 is a beautiful hymn, one that can be used every day of your life to remind you who God is to you, what He promises to do for you, and how much He cares about you.

This is a Psalm of comfort, joy, assurance, and blessing. Let the personal pronouns used by David refer to you, as you lift your heart to the heavenly Shepherd. Let this Psalm become your personal affirmation.

"The Lord is my shepherd; I shall not want" (Ps. 23:1, NKJV). God promises to supply all of your needs, so you will never need to experience want in any form.

"He makes me to lie down in green pastures; He leads me beside the still waters" (Ps. 23:2, NKJV). God will give you rest and peace as you walk with Him.

"He restores my soul; He leads me in the paths of righteousness for His name's sake" (Ps. 23:3, NKJV). God will restore wholeness to your soul, the seat of your emotions, will, and intellect, and He will guide you into all righteousness.

"Yea, though I walk through the valley of the shadow of death, I will fear no evil; for You are with me; Your rod and Your staff, they comfort me" (Ps. 23:4, NKJV). God promises to remove all fear from you, including the fear of death, which is but a shadow when you truly understand and know He is with you. His abiding presence will give you comfort at all times, as you reflect on the fact that God promises eternal life to you.

"You prepare a table before me in the presence of my enemies; You anoint my head with oil; my cup runs over" (Ps. 23:5, NKJV). God will bless you in every conceivable way. He will anoint you with the oil of the Holy Spirit, and you will experience an overflow of His blessings in your life.

"Surely goodness and mercy shall follow me all the days of my life; and I will dwell in the house of the Lord forever" (Ps. 23:6, NKJV). God promises that His goodness and mercy will always be with you, and He will give you everlasting life.

Now turn this Psalm into a personal prayer, as we have done in the following sentences: "Lord God, you are my personal Shepherd. Because this is true, I know I shall never suffer want. Thank you, Father. It is you who makes me lie down in green pastures, and it is you who restores my soul.

"Lead me in the paths of righteousness for your name's sake. Even if I should have to go through the valley of the shadow of death, I know you will be with me. Your rod and your staff will always bring me great comfort.

"Thank you for preparing a table before me in the presence of my enemies. Anoint my head with oil and fill my cup to overflowing. Surely goodness and mercy shall follow me all the days of my life, and I will dwell in your house forever. Thank you, Father, my Shepherd and my God. In Jesus' name I pray, Amen."

As you prayed Psalm 23, we're sure you were reminded of so many truths and promises from the heart of God. This is one of the reasons why praying the Psalms is so important and meaningful.

By praying the Psalms as personal prayers from your heart, and applying them to your personal life and spiritual pilgrimage, you will see God, yourself, others, and all your circumstances in an entirely new light.

The Psalms are filled with God's personal promises to you, His beloved child. As you speak to Him through these powerful passages, He will speak to you. Listen for His voice as you pray, waiting before Him in faith and expectancy.

You are about to discover that the God of the Psalms is your faithful, prayer-answering Father, who loves you with an everlasting love.

The Spiritual Treasury of the Psalms

Major Themes of the Psalms

This chapter takes a look at some of the predominant ideas presented in the Book of Psalms. It is important for you to understand these major themes as you prepare to pray the Psalms, because these concepts are essential to effective prayer and spiritual understanding.

Some of the topics we cover are God's Word, trusting God, thanksgiving and praise, joyful devotion to God, and God's mercy. Each of these is a vital component in the life of faith and prayer, and each is exemplified vividly in the lives of David and the other Psalmists, men who were totally dependent on God.

God's Word – Your Foundation for Life and Prayer

Faith is the key that unlocks the treasure chest known as the Book of Psalms, in which you will find a multitude of shining truths

about God and His ways. The book begins
with a beatitude of blessing that exalts the
importance of the Word of God in the
believer's life: "Blessed is the man that
walketh not in the counsel of the ungodly, nor
standeth in the way of sinners, nor sitteth in
the seat of the scornful. But his delight is in
the law of the Lord; and in his law doth he
meditate day and night" (Ps. 1:1-2).

God promises many things to those who
delight in His Word, and He encourages
believers to meditate therein both night and
day. As you do so, you will receive the
fulfillment of God's promise to you: "And he
shall be like a tree planted by the rivers of
water, that bringeth forth his fruit in his
season; his leaf also shall not wither; and
whatsoever he doeth shall prosper" (Ps. 1:3).

Praying the Psalms shows you how to
meditate in the Word of God (from the Book
of Psalms) at all times, as you personalize and
pray these faith-building Scriptures and apply
them to your life. The end result will be
greater prosperity and fruitfulness in all that
you say and do, including your prayer life.

To learn more about the preeminence of
God's Word, as it is spelled out in the Psalms,
turn to Psalms 19 and 119. In Psalm 19, David
writes, "The law of the Lord is perfect,
converting the soul: the testimony of the Lord

is sure, making wise the simple. The statutes of the Lord are right, rejoicing the heart: the commandment of the Lord is pure, enlightening the eyes" (Ps. 19:7-8).

To David, the Word of God was perfect, sure, right, and pure, and he knew its teachings always bring forth conversion, wisdom, rejoicing, and enlightenment. As you let the life and power of the Bible sink deep within you, these realizations will become a regular part of your daily experience and spiritual understanding.

Pray the Word of God, as it is expressed in the Psalms, and these spiritual treasures will become your personal possession. You will discover the joy of walking in the Word, claiming its promises, and meditating upon its truths.

Indeed, your life will become like that described in Psalm 119: "Blessed are the undefiled in the way, who walk in the law of the Lord. Blessed are they that keep his testimonies, and that seek him with the whole heart. They also do no iniquity: they walk in his ways" (Ps. 119:1-3).

To be blessed is to be happy and to experience the joy of the Lord, which is your strength. (See Neh. 8:10.)

The writer of this Psalm goes on to show how God's Word has the power to keep you from sin and deliver you from shame. He clearly reveres the Word of God, for he recognizes it to be the source of so many spiritual blessings.

He writes, "For ever, O Lord, thy word is settled in heaven. Thy faithfulness is unto all generations" (Ps. 119:89-90).

God's unchanging Word is an anchor for you to hold onto in all the storms and changing seasons of life. By praying the Psalms you are able to rise above life's storms and changing circumstances and to see them from God's perspective.

In God's Word, the Psalmist finds guidance and direction for daily living. He writes, "Thy word is a lamp unto my feet, and a light unto my path" (Ps. 119:105).

He then goes on to say, "Thy word is very pure: therefore thy servant loveth it" (Ps. 119:140).

Love God's Word, and walk in His ways. Let the Psalms provide the substance for many of your prayers, and you will be able to proclaim with the Psalmist, "Great peace have they which love thy law: and nothing shall offend them" (Ps. 119:165).

Likewise, you will be able to pray, "Let my cry come before thee, O Lord: give me understanding according to thy word. Let my supplication come before thee: deliver me according to thy word" (Ps. 119:169-170).

God, your loving Father, will do exactly that. You can always count on Him.

Trusting God

Another major theme we find in the Book of Psalms centers on trusting God. David partially develops this theme in Psalm 5, where he writes, "But let all those rejoice who put their trust in You; let them ever shout for joy, because You defend them; let those also who love Your name be joyful in You. For You, O Lord, will bless the righteous; with favor You will surround him as with a shield" (Ps. 5:11-12, NKJV).

Trusting God leads to the joy of knowing His blessing and favor in your life and that He will always bless you.

True trust in God is assured reliance on His unchanging character, ability, strength, and truth. It is total dependence on God's trustworthiness and faithfulness. Trusting God, then, as David did, is placing unswerving faith in His Word, His promises, His power, His goodness, and His love.

We see this kind of trust and faith revealed in Psalm 20, where David is able to rest and rejoice, because he fully relies on his God. He explains, "Some trust in chariots, and some in horses: but we will remember the name of the Lord our God" (Ps. 20:7-8).

Trusting in God and remembering His name are incomparable spiritual resources for you to draw upon and use in your daily life and prayers.

This truth is similarly brought out in Psalm 31, a great song of trust so beautifully composed by the Psalmist David. He sings, "In thee, O Lord, do I put my trust: let me never be ashamed: deliver me in thy righteousness….For thou art my rock and my fortress; therefore for thy name's sake lead me, and guide me" (Ps. 31:1-3).

David always trusted God to lead and guide him.

Later on, in Psalm 31, David discusses his troubles, which were many. He expresses his grief and sorrow very freely, because he was feeling betrayed, forsaken, and abandoned by his friends and neighbors. In fact, he had become the victim of slander, and certain people were even plotting to assassinate him.

In spite of all these horrendous circumstances and experiences, he was able to write,

"But I trusted in thee, O Lord; I said, Thou art my God. My times are in thy hand: deliver me from the hand of mine enemies, and from them that persecute me" (Ps. 31:14-15).

Through trust, David was able to find peace even in the midst of indescribable danger and turmoil.

This important topic of trust is echoed in Psalms 36 and 37, where David again describes the wicked intentions of his enemies. In the face of their mockery and slander, David writes, "How precious is Your lovingkindness, O God! Therefore the children of men put their trust under the shadow of Your wings.

"They are abundantly satisfied with the fullness of Your house, and You give them drink from the river of Your pleasures. For with You is the fountain of life; in Your light we see light" (Ps. 36:7-9, NKJV).

What are the troubles of this life in comparison to the blessings to be derived from trusting God? David receives a clear answer to this rhetorical question, as he continues to pray.

As if he were counseling himself with God's truth, David's trust in God continues to grow. We see his ability to trust God flower magnificently in Psalm 37, where he writes,

"Fret not thyself because of evildoers, neither be thou envious against the workers of iniquity....Trust in the Lord, and do good: so shalt thou dwell in the land, and verily thou shalt be fed. Delight thyself also in the Lord; and he shall give thee the desires of thine heart.

"Commit thy way unto the Lord; trust also in him; and he shall bring it to pass" (Ps. 37:1-5). The marvelous confidence that is reflected in this passage is the confidence that comes from trusting God implicitly.

Throughout his life, David faced seemingly insurmountable challenges with trust and resolve, and because he did so, he was able to write these words: "But I am like a green olive tree in the house of God: I trust in the mercy of God for ever and ever" (Ps. 52:8).

Trusting God restores the vitality and expectancy of youth to the believer, who places his full confidence and hope in God. In fact, it is a quality of child-like faith.

David was determined to trust God forever. This attitude of his heart culminates in his great hymn of trust in Psalm 91, where he writes: "He that dwelleth in the secret place of the most High shall abide under the shadow of the Almighty. I will say of the Lord, He is my refuge and my fortress: my God; in him will I trust" (Ps. 91:1-2).

This blessed Psalm concludes with several promises from God: "Because he hath set his love upon me, therefore will I deliver him: I will set him on high, because he hath known my name.

"He shall call upon me, and I will answer him: I will be with him in trouble; I will deliver him, and honour him. With long life will I satisfy him, and show him my salvation" (Ps. 91:14-16).

As you trust in Him, God will set you on high. He will always be with you, and He will deliver and honor you. To you, He promises longevity and satisfaction, as the fruit of fully trusting in Him and His Word.

As you embark on the adventure of *Praying the Psalms*, claim this prayer promise as your very own: "He shall call upon me, and I will answer him: I will be with him in trouble; I will deliver him, and honour him" (Ps. 91:15).

Turn this promise into your personal prayer as follows: Father, I thank you for the certain knowledge that, when I call upon you, you will answer me. It's wonderful to know you are always with me, even in times of trouble. Thank you for your promise to deliver me and honor me.

God's Abundant Mercy

The word "mercy" occurs throughout the Book of Psalms. By His wonderful mercy, God shows compassion and forbearance toward His children.

To receive God's mercy is to receive His favor and blessing in your life. God's mercy stems from His great lovingkindness, charity, and grace.

As His child, through faith in Jesus Christ, you are a recipient of God's mercy and grace rather than His judgment and wrath. Because of His great mercy, you are forgiven, redeemed from the enemy, and blessed with eternal life.

These are God's gifts to you, gifts you do not deserve, but they are freely bestowed upon you, because God loves you with an everlasting love.

After David sinned with Bathsheba (See 2 Sam. 11-12.), he prayed to God for mercy. (See Ps. 32.) This is a good example to follow whenever you sin. David prayed, "I acknowledged my sin to You, and my iniquity I have not hidden" (Ps. 32:5, NKJV).

It was an honest confession of sin. God did indeed forgive him, and David was able to proclaim, "Many sorrows shall be to the wicked; but he who trusts in the Lord, mercy shall surround him" (Ps. 32:10, NKJV).

Because he trusted God, mercy had become like a protective shield around the Psalmist, leading him to rejoice in God. He writes, "Be glad in the Lord, and rejoice, ye righteous: and shout for joy" (Ps. 32:11).

Likewise, in the Shepherd's Psalm, David writes, "Surely goodness and mercy shall follow me all the days of my life: and I will dwell in the house of the Lord for ever" (Ps. 23:6). Like the guards on the back of a royal coach in which you are riding, God's goodness and mercy are watching out for you continually.

Many of the Psalms are punctuated with this lovely phrase: "His [God's] mercy endureth for ever." Divine mercy, as it is described in the Psalms, is everlasting, and it is a part of your inheritance as a believer in Jesus Christ.

Notice how the Psalmist develops this concept of God's eternal mercy in Psalm 136: "O give thanks unto the Lord; for he is good: for his mercy endureth for ever. O give thanks unto the God of gods: for his mercy endureth for ever. O give thanks to the Lord of lords: for his mercy endureth for ever.

"To him who alone doeth great wonders: for his mercy endureth for ever. To him that

by wisdom made the heavens: for his mercy
endureth for ever. To him that stretched out
the earth above the waters: for his mercy
endureth for ever. To him that made great
lights: for his mercy endureth for ever" (Ps.
136:1-7).

The Psalms are written in a parallelistic
style, a recurrent literary technique in which
similar sentences are used in juxtaposition to
each other for effect and emphasis. This style
is particularly evident in Psalm 136, where
each thought is buttressed with the persistent
echo: "for his mercy endureth for ever."

In this Psalm, David proclaims specific
truths about God; then he follows each one
with an affirmation of God's eternal mercy.
This beautiful song reminds the believer that
God brought Israel from among the Egyptians
with His strong hand. He divided the Red Sea.

He drowned Pharaoh and his hosts. He
led His people through the wilderness. He
smote great kings. He gave the Promised
Land to His people.

He has redeemed His people from their
enemies. He gives food to all His people. Why
are all these things true? It is simply because
the mercy of God endures forever.

As you pray the Psalms, be sure to reflect
on God's great mercy in your life. Remember

the words of Paul who wrote, "I beseech you therefore, brethren, by the mercies of God, that you present your bodies a living sacrifice, holy, acceptable to God, which is your reasonable service" (Rom. 12:1, NKJV).

Your reasonable service (of worship, honor, and devotion to God) is to give Him your all without holding anything back from Him. Truly, this is the least you can do in light of all His mercies to you.

The Apostle Paul goes on, "And do not be conformed to this world, but be transformed by the renewing of your mind, that you may prove what is that good and acceptable and perfect will of God" (Rom. 12:2, NKJV).

Thanksgiving and Praise

Thanksgiving and praise are two other leading subjects expounded upon throughout the Psalms. In fact, almost every Psalm alludes to this theme in one way or another.

Clearly, the men who wrote the Psalms were very thankful to God for His mercy, grace, and truth, and for all He had done for them personally, and for His people throughout history, in the form of deliverance, protection, provision, forgiveness, and victory.

Many of the Psalms actually are hymns of praise to God, the Father. This may be due largely to the fact that David and the other Psalmists knew the power of prayer, and they loved to sing to their Father. When they asked God for something, they believed they would receive it, and their great faith was always rewarded. They knew God had done it before and He would do it again!

It is clear they knew the truth that was later developed by the writer of Hebrews: "But without faith it is impossible to please him: for he that cometh to God must believe that he is, and that he is a rewarder of them that diligently seek him" (Heb. 11:6).

The men who wrote the Psalms prayed, believed, and received. Therefore, it was natural for them to praise God over and over again.

In Psalm 9, for example, David praises God for victories over enemies, both personal and national. Indeed, he shouts, "I will praise thee, O Lord, with my whole heart; I will show forth all thy marvelous works" (Ps. 9:1).

The victory God gave to David and his people brought forth rejoicing and praise that must have reverberated throughout their land.

Later, in Psalm 18, David thanked God for permitting him to ascend the throne of Israel. This great hymn of thanksgiving expresses immense love to God, and it extols His power and strength.

Throughout Psalm 18, King David reviews the wonderful works of God; how He saved David (and all Israel) from their enemies, how He answered prayer time and time again, how He gave deliverance to David and rewarded him, and how He blessed him in so many ways.

After reminding himself of all these marvelous doings of God, David praises his Father by expressing faith in Him and His ever-present help and protection, "For thou wilt light my candle: the Lord my God will enlighten my darkness. For by thee I have run through a troop; and by my God have I leaped over a wall. As for God, his way is perfect: the word of the Lord is tried: he is a buckler to all those that trust in him" (Ps. 18:28-30).

Praise is the spontaneous response of David's soul as he continues to reflect on all God has done for him. He goes on, "The Lord liveth; and blessed be my rock; and let the God of my salvation be exalted" (Ps. 18:46). Clearly, the Psalmist delighted to praise his Lord, whom he loved with all his heart.

It is not surprising, therefore, that King David concludes this mighty Psalm with praise, "Therefore will I give thanks unto thee, O Lord, among the heathen, and sing praises unto thy name" (Ps. 18:49).

Yes, David is always sure to thank God for everything he can think of, because he knows God as the "Meeter" of every need, the Giver of every good gift, and the Rewarder of faith.

Five other great Psalms of thanksgiving are Psalms 135-139, in which the Psalmist thanks God for His wonderful works in nature and world history, His dealings with Israel, answered prayers, His abiding presence, and His omniscience (His ability to know everything, including our thoughts, needs, and desires).

This glorious theme of praise is picked up again in Psalms 144 and 145, where David expresses resounding praise and thanksgiving to his King. These Psalms are battle hymns, and it may well be that the soldiers in David's army chanted Psalm 144 as they went forth into battle.

If so, their strong, masculine voices praised God in unison as they sang: "Blessed be the Lord my strength, which teacheth my hands to war, and my fingers to fight" (Ps. 144:1).

After the conflicts were over, the soldiers may well have sung Psalm 145, also a battle hymn, after the great victories God gave to them. They rejoiced by singing, "I will extol thee, my God, O king: and I will bless thy name for ever and ever. Every day will I bless thee; and I will praise thy name for ever and ever. Great is the Lord, and greatly to be praised; and his greatness is unsearchable" (Ps. 145:1-3).

The Hebrew word "hallelujah" is used generously in these closing passages of the Book of Psalms, as it is throughout the Bible. It simply means, "Praise [ye] the Lord," and it is both an imperative (a command) and an exclamatory heart cry that issues from the soul of everyone who knows how good God is.

Because praise and thanksgiving are such dominant themes within the Book of Psalms, it is fitting that the final Psalm is a marvelous paean (a joyously exultant hymn of praise, tribute, thanksgiving, and triumph) to God. "Praise ye the Lord. Praise God in his sanctuary: praise him in the firmament of his power. Praise him for his mighty acts: praise him according to his excellent greatness. Praise him with the sound of the trumpet: praise him with the psaltery and harp.

"Praise him with the timbrel and dance: praise him with stringed instruments and organs. Praise him upon the loud cymbals: praise him upon the high sounding cymbals. Let every thing that hath breath praise the Lord. Praise ye the Lord" (Ps. 150).

Hallelujah!

Joyful Devotion to God

Throughout the ages, believers have expressed their faith and their joyful devotion to God through songs, hymns, psalms, and happy service. This is not surprising, because God has always proven himself faithful to each one.

We see this attitude of joyful devotion reflected in Psalm 33: "Rejoice in the Lord, O ye righteous: for praise is comely for the upright....Sing unto him a new song; play skillfully with a loud noise" (Ps. 33:1-3).

A new song was necessary because God had done a new thing for His people and this resulted in new joy and deeper devotion to the Lord.

David danced with joy before the Lord, because he realized so completely all that God had done for him. Psalm 40 reveals one of the reasons why David was so joyful in his devotion to God. "I waited patiently for the Lord; and he inclined unto me, and heard my cry.

"He brought me up also out of an horrible pit, out of the miry clay, and set my feet upon a rock, and established my goings. And he hath put a new song in my mouth, even praise unto our God: many shall see it, and fear, and shall trust in the Lord" (Ps. 40:1-3).

In Psalm 96, David turns this thought into an imperative, a mandate for God's people everywhere: "O sing unto the Lord a new song: sing unto the Lord, all the earth. Sing unto the Lord, bless his name; show forth his salvation from day to day" (Ps. 96:1-2).

Why should believers sing? It is because God has done so much for His children. Like the ancient Hebrews, the Church of Jesus Christ is a singing company of people. Believers sing because they're happy, and they sing because they're joyful; happy and joyful, because God has done so much for each one and for His people, collectively, as well.

We see this joyful, faith-filled singing advocated by the Psalmist again in Psalm 98: "O sing unto the Lord a new song; for he hath done marvelous things: his right hand, and his holy arm, hath gotten him the victory....Make a joyful noise unto the Lord, all the earth: make a loud noise, and rejoice, and sing praise. Sing unto the Lord" (Ps. 98:1-5).

Perhaps the best Psalm to look at with regard to the theme of joyful devotion is Psalm 100, a God-glorifying hymn of praise: "Make a joyful noise unto the Lord, all ye lands. Serve the Lord with gladness: come before his presence with singing. Know ye that the Lord he is God: it is he that hath made us, and not we ourselves; we are his people, and the sheep of his pasture.

"Enter into his gates with thanksgiving, and into his courts with praise: be thankful unto him, and bless his name. For the Lord is good; his mercy is everlasting; and his truth endureth to all generations" (Ps. 100).

The Psalmist commands believers everywhere to serve the Lord with gladness. This is joyful devotion to God.

Such service must never be done grudgingly or with the heaviness that comes from serving simply from a sense of duty. Rather, it is done with joy, because each believer recognizes the truth of Nehemiah's words: "The joy of the Lord is my strength" (Neh. 8:10).

Truly spiritual joy emanates from the sense of well-being, success, victory, and blessing that each one who knows God enjoys. This kind of joyful devotion is what the Apostle Peter refers to when he writes, "That the trial of your faith, being much more precious than of gold that perisheth, though it be tried with fire, might be found unto praise and honour and glory at the appearing of Jesus Christ: whom having not seen, ye love; in whom, though now ye see him not, yet believing, ye rejoice with joy unspeakable and full of glory" (1 Pet. 1:7-8).

Singing is a unique art form that enables us to express the joyful, spiritual pulses that surge from every believer's heart as a result of a personal relationship with God. It has been an integral part of the life of God's people from ancient times to the present.

The Old Testament books of Exodus and Deuteronomy disclose that Moses sang, and he led his people in singing as well. This preparation for joyful service caused the Israelites to sing as they journeyed to the Promised Land. (See Num. 21:17.)

The Bible says that David was committed to singing unto God throughout all his life. This is vividly expressed in one of his affirmations of joyful devotion to God: "I will sing unto the Lord as long as I live: I will sing praise to my God while I have my being. My meditation of him shall be sweet: I will be glad in the Lord" (Ps. 104:33-34).

It is good to learn to sing with joyful devotion to God in this life, because in heaven everyone will sing, along with all the angels. John writes this description of the heavenly chorus: "And I beheld, and I heard the voice of many angels round about the throne and the beasts and the elders: and the number of them was ten thousand times ten thousand, and thousands of thousands;

"Saying with a loud voice, worthy is the Lamb that was slain to receive power, and riches, and wisdom, and strength, and honour, and glory, and blessing" (Rev. 5:11-12).

Joyful devotion to God entails loving Him, serving Him, and expressing praise and honor to Him in worship, witnessing, service, and private times of prayer and communion. It is exciting and energizing. In fact, it is a vital part of your prayer life.

As you learn to pray the Psalms, you will be inspired to engage in joyful devotion to God, your heavenly Father, each day of your life. In so doing, you will find that your greatest joy in life is to serve God in everything you do. This will cause your spirit to soar, and you will want to sing and rejoice as the Psalmists did so many centuries ago.

"Great is the Lord, and greatly to be praised in the city of our God, in the mountain of his holiness….For this God is our God for ever and ever: he will be our guide even unto death" (Ps. 48).

Understanding Key Concepts in the Psalms

Understanding the Law in the Psalms

**Five Meanings of "Law"
in the Old Testament**

The word "law," as it is used in the Old Testament, is sometimes ambiguous because it has multiple meanings. One of its meanings is concerned with God's revelation in general. This includes His written revelation (the Word of God), as well as His revelation in nature.

Often, the Psalmists used the word "law" to refer to God's revelation in general, and they may employ synonyms, such as "ordinances," "statutes," "precepts," "commandments," and "judgments" in doing so.

Another definition of the word, "law" as it is used in the Old Testament, refers to the five books of Moses known as the Pentateuch (Genesis, Exodus, Leviticus, Numbers, and Deuteronomy).

In these first five books of the Bible, Moses transcribes God's law that has since come to be known as the Mosaic Code, Mosaic Law, or Mosaic system.

The Mosaic Code includes the Ten Commandments Moses received from God on Mount Sinai, along with specific laws regarding human behavior, religious rituals, moral requirements, and social standards.

This leads us to a third way in which the word "law" may have been intended in Old Testament times, as a reference to specific instructions and commandments the Israelites were expected to follow. These laws concerned such things as slavery, death for murder, kindness to widows and orphans, etc.

Another way in which the word "law" was understood in Old Testament times regards instructions related to ceremonial regulations concerning religious rituals and practices. This sense of the word "law" might refer to matters related to observing the Sabbath, ritual cleansing, etc.

In addition, the Law of Moses was insistent with regard to social and moral standards for the Israelites. This is the fifth way in which the word "law" is understood in the Old Testament.

These strict standards govern personal morality, as well as consideration for old people, children, animals, slaves, and enemies. It also included regulations regarding food, cleanliness, and health.

The Law of God, in all five of the senses mentioned, was meant to show the Israelites how to live in covenant with their Lord. The Old Testament, and its emphasis on law, was based on God's will, and it clearly demonstrated His love for His children. God gave them the Law to lead them to greater happiness and fulfillment. (See Deut. 10:12-13.)

Our Faithful, Covenant-Keeping God

It was God's will to establish a special redemptive relationship with His people. In order to do so, He inspired Moses to formalize His desires for Israel in the form of a legal covenant and/or contract.

Essentially, the Mosaic Code thus prepared was a system of rewards and punishments related to the individual's obedience or disobedience to the laws of God.

Much earlier, when God had revealed himself to the patriarch, Abraham, He had established a covenant with him. The divine promise was that in Abraham's seed all nations would be blessed.

This was God's promise to Abraham and it was one of His reasons for founding the Jewish nation and religion. How would all the nations be blessed through Abraham? A Messiah would come forth from this nation to save people from their sins.

The Hebrews, as a result of the Abrahamic Covenant, therefore, did have a relationship with God. When the Law came, it revealed to the Jews how they could experience fellowship with God, their Father, who had established an eternal covenant with them that was based on His love for them. Through the Law they were enabled to experience fellowship with their Father in heaven, to know His love more fully, and to express their love to Him.

The essence of God's covenant with the Hebrew nation was that, if they would serve Him faithfully, they would prosper as a nation, but, if they forsook Him and His ways, they would surely be punished.

The Israelite's failure to keep both the Law and their part of the covenant agreement caused great havoc to come upon them for many years. For example, they were enslaved by the Egyptians and had to wander in the wilderness for forty years.

When their nation was reestablished, however, God entered into a new covenant relationship with their king, David, that his family should reign over God's people. He also promised that, from David's lineage, a Messianic King would come forth to bring salvation to those who would believe in Him and to establish an eternal kingdom.

God had revealed himself as a covenant-keeping God through the covenants he had established with Abraham, Moses, and David.

Faith and Love in the Law

It is important to realize that the Law, as given by God to the nation of Israel, was not, even for them, just a set of rules to be kept. It also set forth God's guidelines for how to walk in love toward each other and to express their love to God.

The Law of God was a revelation of His goodness, love, holiness, and grace. It is important to understand, however, that the Jews were not saved by keeping the Law.

Like New Testament believers, the Israelites were saved by and through faith. Hebrews 11, in referring to Old Testament saints, declares: "These all died in faith, not having received the promises, but having seen them afar off were assured of them, embraced them and confessed that they were strangers and pilgrims on the earth" (Heb. 11:13, NKJV).

Paul helps us understand how faith was effective in the Old Testament believer's life. He writes, "For if Abraham was justified by works, he has something to boast about, but not before God. For what does the Scripture say? 'Abraham believed God, and it was accounted unto him for righteousness'" (Rom. 4:2-3, NKJV).

Jesus Fulfilled the Law

As a Jew, Jesus lived under the Law, and He obeyed it. His mission was not to destroy the Law, but to fulfill it, and He did so by teaching believers that God is not only concerned with a person's outward behaviors, but with the attitudes and motives of the heart.

Jesus' Sermon on the Mount (See Matt. 5-7.) helps us to understand how He fulfilled the Law by showing us that the Law is not God's way to complete sanctification and holiness, but it is more like a mirror in which we see our inadequacy for keeping the Law and our need for forgiveness vividly reflected.

Jesus did, however, reject the extra-canonical, man-made rules that Jewish leaders had imposed upon their people.

He said, "Unless your righteousness exceeds the righteousness of the scribes and Pharisees, you will by no means enter the kingdom of heaven" (Matt. 5:20, NKJV).

In saying this, Jesus was teaching that the scribes and Pharisees, who may have tried to keep the Law as fully as possible, were totally unable to gain God's approval in this way. They thought they were righteous, but they had failed to understand the weakness of human flesh and their need for a Savior, who would cleanse them from all unrighteousness.

In fact, Jesus called them, "whited sepulchers," indicating that their righteousness was only on the surface; it did not change their hearts.

Law Versus Grace in the New Testament

Throughout the New Testament, the word "law" may be understood to refer to many different concepts, including those covered by the Old Testament, as well as new concepts presented in God's New Covenant with his people.

Through the Law, we gain insight into God's justice — His concern for every human being.

We also see the importance of sacrifice in the Law. The purpose of sacrifice is to invite the sinner to experience God's grace.

Intermingled with the Law are God's promises to His people. The rules He established for them were meant to help them live holy and happy lives.

In short, God revealed His holy, loving character to His people through the Law. He also taught them something else; that they were ill-equipped to keep His law. When one truly understood this, he would lean more on faith rather than on works.

Paul writes, "Therefore by the deeds of the law no flesh will be justified in His sight, for by the law is the knowledge of sin" (Rom. 3:20, NKJV).

The Law cannot produce the righteousness it demands from its adherents. Rather, it exposes their sinfulness and weakness, and sometime even stimulates man's sinful nature. We may see this force at work in the lives of children whose parents tell them not to do something, such as to take a cookie from the cookie jar. The prohibition opens the door to the temptation to disobey.

This is what Adam and Eve experienced in the Garden of Eden, when God told them not to eat of the fruit of the tree of the knowledge of good and evil. The temptation to disobey overwhelmed them and, as a result, the law of sin and death invaded the human race.

The Law of God serves to point human beings in the direction of grace. Paul wrote, "But before faith came, we were kept under the law, kept for the faith which would be afterward revealed. Therefore the law was our tutor to bring us to Christ, that we might be justified by faith" (Gal. 3:23-24, NKJV).

The Law, as our schoolmaster, taught us that, no matter how well we performed, we could not even come close to gaining salvation, "for all have sinned and fall short of the glory of God" (Rom. 3:23, NKJV).

The Law, as it was transcribed by Moses, was only a temporary expedient, which was to be replaced by a higher law, in God's good time.

Paul wrote, "There is therefore now no condemnation to those who are in Christ Jesus....For the law of the Spirit of life in Christ Jesus has made me free from the law of sin and death" (Rom 8:1-2, NKJV).

He further elaborates on this aspect of the New Covenant as follows: "For what the law could not do in that it was weak through the flesh, God did by sending His own Son in the likeness of sinful flesh, on account of sin: He condemned sin in the flesh, that the righteous requirement of the law might be fulfilled in us who do not walk according to the flesh but according to the Spirit" (Rom. 8:3-4, NKJV).

The death of Jesus Christ introduced an entirely new approach to working out the believer's faith relationship with God. This led Paul to announce that we are no longer under law, but under grace. He wrote, "For sin shall not have dominion over you, for you are not under law but under grace" (Rom 6:14, NKJV).

God's grace, as it is revealed through Jesus Christ, enables us to what we could not do, be what we could not be, and receive what we could not receive, including salvation, righteousness, and holiness. "For the wages of sin is death, but the gift of God is eternal life in Christ Jesus our Lord" (Rom. 6:23, NKJV).

Paul is careful to point out, however, that being under grace rather than law does not mean that the believer is free from the obligation to live righteously before God. (See Rom. 6:15-18.)

It is the sacrificial death of Christ — the unblemished Lamb of God — that releases God's people from the bondage the Law had imposed upon us. No matter how hard one may have tried to obey all the laws found in the Mosaic system, the individual was doomed to failure, because he or she was never able to attain to righteousness in such a way. (See Rom. 7:1-25.)

Unfortunately, sometimes New Testament believers are misled into thinking that legalism (keeping laws) and good works will save them and help them to be righteous. This is a snare the enemy has laid for them, for no matter how hard they strive, struggle, and strain to make themselves acceptable to God, they reap only a sense of greater condemnation and frustration.

Therefore, the believer who tries to relate to God through the old system, by endeavoring to keep the rules perfectly, will always fail. Paul writes, "For sin, taking occasion by the commandment deceived me" (Rom. 7:11, NKJV).

On the other hand, the believer who relates to God in the way outlined by the New Covenant will discover that the righteous requirements of the Law will be fully met in his or her life by faith in Jesus Christ, who is the Righteous One, and by yielding to the power of the Holy Spirit.

How wonderful it is to be a New Covenant believer through faith in Jesus Christ. We no longer have to wait, as the Psalmists did, for a promised hope, for we are children of a better covenant established on better promises, secured for us through the precious shed blood of Christ, our Savior. Do you know Him? Would like to?

If you do not know Jesus as your own personal Savior and would like to, just pray this simple prayer of faith and surrender to Him: "Jesus, I receive you as my personal Savior and Lord. I ask you to come into my heart right now and make me new. I surrender all to you and ask you to be the Lord of my life now and forever. I confess my sins to you, and I ask you to forgive me and cleanse me from all unrighteousness. I believe you died for my sins and that you have been raised from the dead by God, the Father, and the power of the Holy Spirit. I now confess with my mouth that I believe these things and that you are my Lord. I am now your child. I am a member of the family of God, a partaker of your New Covenant. According to your Word, I am a new creation. I have been born again. Thank you, Jesus, my Lord. Amen."

Jesus, Our Righteousness

Paul writes, "But of Him you are in Christ Jesus, who became for us wisdom from God — and righteousness and sanctification and redemption — that, as it is written, 'He who glories, let him glory in the Lord'" (1 Cor. 1:30-31, NKJV).

Jesus Christ is our way to righteousness, sanctification, and redemption, and through the power of the Holy Spirit, we are able to resist the sinful passions of our flesh and do the will of God. (See Rom. 8:5-15.)

The Role of the Holy Spirit

The infilling of the Holy Spirit in the believer's life is a great key to spiritual victory, for His indwelling presence manifests in the form of spiritual fruit in the believer's life.

The young church at Galatia had come under the influence of a sect of people known as the Judaizers. These Jewish believers insisted that Christians had to come to God through Judaism first. They believed that even Gentiles must become Jews and keep the Jewish law before they could become true Christians.

Paul was adamant in his stand against such a preposterous idea. He wrote, "Stand fast therefore in the liberty by which Christ has made us free, and not be entangled again with a yoke of bondage" (Gal. 5:1, NKJV).

He further explained, "Walk in the Spirit, and you shall not fulfill the lust of the flesh....If you are led by the Spirit, you are not under the law" (Gal. 5:16-18, NKJV).

The Great Apostle proceeds to contrast the works of the flesh with the fruit of the Spirit.

He defines the fruit of the Spirit as follows: "But the fruit of the Spirit is love, joy, peace, longsuffering, kindness, goodness, faithfulness, gentleness, self-control" (Gal. 5:22-23, NKJV).

Notice his resounding conclusion to this passage: "Against such there is no law" (Gal. 5:23, NKJV).

Law, and Praying the Psalms

People of faith in the Old Testament obeyed the Law out of love for God and an awareness of His great love for them.

For example, when the Psalmists had sinned and offered their sacrifices in faith, they knew that they would be restored to fellowship with God. Similarly, when they went to God in faith, seeking His protection, healing, deliverance, or strength, they knew that God had promised to meet their needs and would always take care of them.

Now you understand how it was that the Psalmists could say they loved God's law. (See Ps. 119:97, 127.)

As you pray the Psalms and encounter references to the Law, remember the major points of the history we've just outlined, and rejoice in the fact that you are no longer under the Old Testament concept of law, but under grace. Keep in mind the fact that the Law was your schoolmaster; it served to bring you to the grace imparted by and through Jesus Christ.

"For by grace you have been saved through faith, and that not of yourselves; it is the gift of God, not of works, lest anyone should boast" (Eph. 2:8-9, NKJV).

Finally, keep ever before you these words of Paul: "For all the law is fulfilled in one word, even in this: 'You shall love your neighbor as yourself'" (Gal. 5:14, NKJV), and again, "Love does no harm to a neighbor; therefore love is the fulfillment of the law" (Rom. 13:10, NKJV).

In the commandment Jesus called the greatest of all, "You shall love the Lord your God with all your heart, with all your soul, and with all your mind" (Matt: 22:37, NKJV), and the one he called second and like it, "You shall love your neighbor as yourself" (Matt. 22:39, NKJV), you see the ultimate goal of the Law as love.

Now you are ready to pray the Psalms with powerful insight and a clearer understanding of terms you will encounter which refer to the Law.

Understanding the Temple of God in the Psalms

The Temple of God, to Old Testament believers, was a place of worship, but it was far more than that as well. To them, the Temple was where God dwelled — His place of dwelling, His abode, His house.

David proclaimed, "One thing have I desired of the Lord, that will I seek: that I may dwell in the house of the Lord all the days of my life, to behold the beauty of the Lord, and to inquire in His temple" (Ps. 27:4, NKJV). The foremost thing David sought with all his heart was to dwell in God's presence and to behold His beauty throughout his life.

He knew this would result in great blessing for him, for he wrote, "For in the time of trouble He shall hide me in His pavilion; in the secret place of His tabernacle He shall hide me; He shall set me high upon a rock" (Ps. 27:5, NKJV).

The words "temple," "tabernacle," and "pavilion" that we see in Psalm 27 (and throughout the Psalms) are words that represent God's presence. Therefore, as you pray the Psalms and encounter these words, remember that you are seeking more of God's presence in your life.

In His presence, we experience joy, peace, fulfillment, healing, restoration, deliverance, blessing, and intimacy with God. For these reasons and many more, the Israelites, as the Psalmists revealed, sought the dwelling-place of God with all their hearts.

For 400 years, God's dwelling-place was a special tent known as the Tabernacle. Later, the glorious Temple of Solomon was built in order to be a more permanent house of God, but it remained standing for only five years after King Solomon's death.

In New Testament times, Herod's Temple was erected in glory to God. This was the Temple which Christ visited as a young adolescent and at various times during His earthly ministry. It was a truly magnificent edifice that was destroyed by the Romans in AD 70.

Jesus referred to His own body as a temple. (See John 2:19-21.) He taught us that temple buildings are not necessary for worshiping God, and that we can experience God's presence wherever we go.

He explained this to the woman at the well who expressed great confusion over the appropriate place for worshiping God.

Jesus said, "Woman, believe Me, the hour is coming when you will neither on this mountain, nor in Jerusalem, worship the Father....But the hour is coming, and now is, when the true worshipers will worship the Father in spirit and truth; for the Father is seeking such to worship Him. God is Spirit, and those who worship Him must worship in spirit and truth" (John 4:21-24, NKJV).

Paul discloses that the Church of Jesus Christ is God's temple, His dwelling-place in the world. (See 1 Cor. 3:16-19.)

Similarly, each believer in Jesus Christ is God's temple as well. Paul reveals this truth to us in his first letter to the Corinthians: "Or do you not know that your body is the temple of the Holy Spirit who is in you, whom you have from God, and you are not your own? For you were bought with a price; therefore glorify God in your body and in your spirit, which are God's" (1 Cor. 6:19-20, NKJV).

The New Testament discusses, also, the Temple in heaven as God's dwelling-place. (See Rev. 11:19.)

Remember, then, as you pray the Psalms, that all references to the Temple represent the place where God maintained His abode. Today, these references point us, as New Testament believers, to God as present in His heavenly tabernacle, and also to His glorious presence both with us and in us. We open the door to His presence through faith in Jesus Christ.

For example, if you personalize Psalm 138:1-2 as a prayer, you will enter, enjoy, and experience God's presence. As you do so, you will pray words similar to these: "I will praise You with my whole heart....I will worship toward Your holy temple, and praise Your name for Your lovingkindness and Your truth; for You have magnified Your word above all Your name" (Ps. 138:1-2, NKJV).

To sum up, for us today, to worship toward God's holy temple is to come boldly to His throne of grace (the place of His presence) and worship Him in spirit and in truth. Then we will experience His presence, His power, His glory, and His love. This is the place of blessing and joy, as David declares in Psalm 16: "You will show me the path of life; in Your presence is fullness of joy; at Your right hand are pleasures forevermore" (Ps. 16:11, NKJV).

Understanding Zion in the Psalms

Zion is the city of God, and it may be taken to refer to the holy city of Jerusalem, the Church of Jesus Christ, or the heavenly city, which John describes in the Revelation. Whatever the case, it is a place where God lives.

Jerusalem was built on the ridge of a mountain, and it was surrounded by deep valleys. King David selected Jerusalem to be the capital of Israel in 1000 BC.

The Psalmist wrote, "Great is the Lord, and greatly to be praised in the city of our God, in His holy mountain. Beautiful in elevation, the joy of the whole earth, is Mount Zion on the sides of the north, the city of the great King. God is in her palaces; He is known as her refuge" (Ps. 48:1-3, NKJV).

In this Psalm, the sons of Korah describe the city of God — Jerusalem — as a most beautiful place situated high atop a mountain. It is a place of God's dwelling, and it is a place of refuge, which, because of its elevation, is not easily accessible to enemies.

The Psalmists and the prophets often speak of Zion in a prophetic sense as well, pointing to the New Testament church and the city of God in heaven. Zechariah does so as he writes: "Thus says the Lord: 'I will return to Zion, and dwell in the midst of Jerusalem. Jerusalem shall be called the City of Truth, the Mountain of the Lord of hosts, the Holy Mountain'" (Zech. 8:3, NKJV).

The prophet continues, "Behold, I will save My people from the land of the east and from the land of the west; I will bring them back, and they shall dwell in the midst of Jerusalem. They shall be My people and I will be their God, in truth and righteousness" (Zech. 8:7-8, NKJV).

In the New Testament, the writer of Hebrews make a direct comparison between Zion, the Church of Jesus Christ, and the heavenly city when he writes, "But you have come to Mount Zion and to the city of the living God, the heavenly Jerusalem, to an innumerable company of angels, to the general assembly and church of the firstborn who are registered in heaven…" (Heb. 12:22-23, NKJV).

With these thoughts in mind, as you are praying a passage from the Psalms that refers to Zion, be sure to remember that the city of God is the place of God's dwelling, the New Testament church, and a preview of the heavenly city toward which each believer is journeying.

Understanding Blessing God in the Psalms

Did it ever occur to you that you can actually bless God as you pray? Every believer knows how God blesses His people, but what does blessing God mean and how may we do so?

A blessing is an act that gladdens the heart of its recipient, pleases him/her, and causes him/her to take delight in the one who bestows the blessing.

God, our loving heavenly Father, takes great delight in you when you bless Him through worship and praise. Indeed, it thrills His heart to receive the blessing of His children's love being expressed to Him. Therefore, as you honor and reverence Him in prayer and adoration, God is truly blessed.

The Psalmists loved to bless God, as the following verse clearly shows: "Bless the Lord, O my soul! O Lord God, You are very great: You are clothed with honor and majesty" (Ps. 104:1, NKJV).

To bless God, as the Psalmists did, is to honor and glorify God for everything He has done for You and for who He is to you. As you pray the Psalms, you will be blessing God, and He will take great delight in you, His beloved child.

Understanding the Fear of the Lord in the Psalms

The expression "the fear of the Lord" is found, not only in the Psalms, but throughout the Bible, and refers to the reverential awe which leads the believer to love and obey God.

In the sense we find it used in Psalm 34:11, it might be considered a definition of "true religion." "Come, you children, listen to me; I will teach you the fear of the Lord" (NKJV).

When we find, as in Proverbs 1:7, the statement, "The fear of the Lord is the beginning of knowledge," it might be said to mean that a solemn respect for the living God is the underpinning of all spiritual faith and morality.

The nature and result of a reverential awe of God is set forth in Deuteronomy 10:12-13. Here, God commands Israel to fear Him, equating such fear with the way of life and the heart attitudes it produces. "And now, Israel, what does the Lord your God require of you, but to fear the Lord your God, to walk in all His ways and to love Him, to serve the Lord your God with all your heart and with all your soul, and to keep the commandments of the Lord and His statutes which I command you today for your good" (NKJV).

The New Testament also reflects a reverent awe of God as the motive for holy living. The one who truly fears the Lord has an awareness of His power and authority, which produces a godly life. As the writer of Hebrews 12:28-29 says, "Therefore, since we are receiving a kingdom which cannot be shaken, let us have grace, by which we may serve God acceptably with reverence and

godly fear. For our God is a consuming fire"
(NKJV).

Self-satisfaction and rebellion might be
seen as valid antonyms for the fear of the Lord.
Paul uses the term "fear," for example, in his
letter to the Philippians: "…work out your own
salvation with fear and trembling" (Phil. 2:12).

God has established the way of
redemption and salvation. It is our reverence
for Him and His awesome love that leads us
to the Way. Without such fear and trembling
in our hearts toward both God's goodness
and His judgment, we will satisfy ourselves
with our own goodness and reject His plan of
salvation and the blessing that accompanies
being His children.

God's judgment is greatly to be feared, if
the awesomeness of both His love and His
holiness have never been revealed to us.

It is in this sense that the Psalmists use the
expression, and it is with this understanding
that we should read and pray, not only the
Psalms, but the entire Bible.

Understanding the Concepts of Vindication and Revenge in the Psalms

From a New Testament perspective, it
sometimes seems as if the Psalmists are

particularly vindictive and vengeful in their prayers, especially regarding their enemies. The Psalms that focus on such desires for retribution and vindication are known as imprecatory Psalms.

The main imprecatory Psalms are Psalms 35, 52, 58, 59, 69, 109, and 137. As Christians, we may sometimes find these Psalms to be jarring and troublesome in that they appear to stand in opposition to Christ's teachings about loving our enemies and praying for them.

As you pray these Psalms, we suggest that you view them in the context of the times in which they were written. Understand that many of these prayers are actually patriotic hymns to inspire the nation of Israel to take a strong stand against their enemies.

In so doing, you may wish to give these Psalms a spiritual application as well. Turn them into personal prayers against the enemy, Satan, and his evil emissaries in this world of darkness.

Using the imprecatory Psalms in this way will help you to engage in effective spiritual warfare, as you remember that the Word of God is the sword of the Spirit that you can wield against the enemy to gain victory in your own life. (See Eph. 6:10-17.)

As you fight the good fight of faith, "Be strong in the Lord and in the power of His might" (Eph. 6:10, NKJV), remembering that "...we do not wrestle against flesh and blood, but against principalities, against the rulers of the darkness of this age, against spiritual hosts of wickedness in the heavenly places" (Eph. 6:12, NKJV).

Understanding the Concept of Emotional Healing in the Psalms

A powerful way to read and pray the Psalms is to open your heart to the thoughts, feelings, and emotions expressed by the Psalmists.

This is a very practical and healing thing to do, because many of the Psalms address our most difficult times, the times when we find ourselves in the grip of strong and often tormenting feelings and emotions.

Thus, praying the Psalms can lead us through a healing process of our own, similar to that of the Psalmists. During difficult circumstances, as they cried out for God's deliverance, and they saw their own sin, God helped them see, also, that salvation and deliverance could only come from Him. In this way they were able to experience His healing love.

The Psalms show us how to openly and honestly express our emotions and life experiences to our loving heavenly Father, knowing He will hear us and meet our needs. Praying the Psalms will bring us to the place of inner peace and contentment the Psalmists consistently found.

When you pray the passages from the Psalms dealing with personal problems and times of trouble, look inward, examine your heart honestly before God, and seek to understand the true source of the difficulties you are experiencing.

As you do so, God will reveal to you each step you need to take in order to experience the healing, wholeness, and victory He has in store for you. Or He may miraculously give you what you need in that very moment of prayer.

When you are praying the passages from the Psalms that deal with victory, joy, healing, deliverance, adoration, and praise, enter fully into the exciting and fulfilling exultation experienced by the Psalmists during their times of great gladness and triumph. This will enable you to worship in both humility and freedom along with the Psalmists.

The Men Who Wrote
the Psalms

The Psalmists

There are 150 Psalms in the Bible. David wrote seventy-three of these. The other Psalmists are Asaph (who wrote twelve Psalms), the sons of Korah (who wrote eleven), Solomon (who wrote two), Moses (who wrote one), and Ethan (who wrote one).

Fifty of the Psalms are anonymous, but many believe that the individuals who wrote the Psalms immediately preceding the ones without attribution authored them as well.

In this chapter we take a brief look at the lives of the men who wrote the Psalms in an effort to discover how their faith and experiences wove together to turn them into some of the greatest poets and songwriters of all time. Clearly, they were also men of great faith and wisdom.

The Psalter provides us with fine works of art that are truly classical, both with regard to the ancient times in which they were written and the eternal magnificence of their truth and beauty.

W.E. Gladstone, a British statesman and Prime Minister of Great Britain during the Victorian Era, wrote, "All the wonders of Greek civilization heaped together are less wonderful than is this simple Book of the Psalms."

We concur with his statement, because we know the Psalms to be a rich treasury of artistic beauty, spiritual and prophetic insight, and intense devotion to God from which we have learned so much about faith and prayer.

Asaph

King David placed Asaph in charge of the "service of the song" in the Tabernacle. He was the founder of one of the three chief families or guilds of Levite temple worship.

Asaph, it is believed, wrote Psalm 50, a marvelous Psalm in which this anointed song leader gave great honor to God through praise and reflection upon His marvelous works.

He writes, "Whoso offereth praise glorifieth me: and to him that ordereth his conversation aright will I show the salvation of God" (Ps. 50:23). Asaph loved to praise

God, and he always encouraged the Israelites to do the same.

He also wrote Psalm 73, in which he reminds Israel of God's great goodness to them. In this hymn he discusses the wickedness of evildoers at some length, and concludes, "Whom have I in heaven but thee? And there is none upon earth that I desire beside thee. My flesh and my heart faileth: but God is the strength of my heart, and my portion for ever….But it is good for me to draw near to God: I have put my trust in the Lord God, that I may declare all thy works" (Ps. 73:25-28).

In Psalm 74, Asaph begins with the voice of despair by saying, "O God, why hast thou cast us off for ever? Why doth thine anger smoke against the sheep of thy pasture?" (Ps. 74:1).

By the end of this Psalm, however, in characteristic fashion, the musician reminds himself and all God's people of His unparalleled goodness.

He writes, "For God is my King of old, working salvation in the midst of the earth" (Ps. 74:12). Asaph was able to identify with people who felt that God had forgotten them or was angry with them.

In the next Psalm written by Asaph (Psalm 75), we hear him singing with increasing confidence as he extols the greatness of God. He writes, "Unto thee, O God, do we give thanks, unto thee do we give thanks: for that thy name is near thy wondrous works declare" (Ps. 75:1).

Asaph recognizes the sovereignty of God as he reminds us, "For promotion cometh neither from the east, nor from the west, nor from the south. But God is the judge: he putteth down one, and setteth up another" (Ps. 75:6-7).

In Psalm 76, we read these inspired words of Asaph in further praise of God: "Thou art more glorious and excellent than the mountains of prey" (Ps. 76:4).

That Asaph loved God is evident in all his writings. He writes, "Thou art the God that doest wonders: thou hast declared thy strength among the people" (Ps. 77:14). To Asaph, God was a Miracle-worker whose strength enabled Him to do all things.

Psalm 78 is a maschil of Asaph. A maschil is a particular kind of Psalm that would have been accompanied by special kinds of music and was probably sung at a special festival, perhaps an annual holiday.

This particular maschil reminds Israel of the mighty works God did for them throughout history, such as the provision of manna as they wandered in the wilderness and the gushing waters that miraculously flowed from the rock.

Asaph also shows how the disobedience of the wandering Hebrews eventually provoked God's wrath, causing Him to discipline them with hardships of various kinds.

God forgave them, however, and His mercy prevailed over His justice.

This led the Psalmist Asaph to conclude his hymn with these words, "So he fed them according to the integrity of his heart; and guided them by the skillfulness of his hands" (Ps. 78:72).

In Psalm 79, Asaph asks for God's help and defense against the enemies of Israel. This, he concludes, will enable the people to "...give thee thanks for ever: we will show forth thy praise to all generations" (Ps. 79:13).

He continues these themes in Psalm 80, where he writes, "Turn us again, O Lord God of hosts, cause thy face to shine; and we shall be saved" (Ps. 80:19).

Another great song of Asaph is found in Psalm 81. First, the great hymnist encourages God's people to praise God with many kinds of musical instruments (timbrels, harps, and trumpets).

Then Asaph takes on a prophetic tone as he writes, "I am the Lord thy God, which brought thee out of the land of Egypt: open thy mouth wide, and I will fill it" (Ps. 81:10).

Ever mindful of God's faithfulness and miracle-working power, this Psalmist is always careful to show God's people why they need to praise Him at all times.

Psalm 82, another of Asaph's psalms, is a very short prayer to God as the Judge. In this Psalm, he prays, "Arise, O God, judge the earth: for thou shalt inherit all nations" (Ps. 82:8). He pleads for the poor, orphans, sick people, and others who need God's mercy.

Psalm 83 is a song that was written by Asaph in order to ask God for His protection and deliverance from the enemies of Israel, that people everywhere would know He is God.

He writes, "That men may know that thou, whose name alone is Jehovah, art the most high over all the earth" (Ps. 83:18).

Though Asaph wrote only twelve of the Psalms, his contributions to the Psalter must never be discounted or minimized, for he honors God in a most compelling manner that is a great model for each believer to follow.

He loves God and praises Him, because he knows God as the One who is ever-present to help His children get through any difficulties that may come their way. His call to praise and thanksgiving resounds joyfully within the hearts of all God's children.

The Sons of Korah

Like Asaph, the sons of Korah were singers and song leaders in the Temple. It appears that they were leaders and members of a great choir. These brothers led the people of God in worship through inspired music and choral interpretations.

Though we don't know their individual names, we know their ministry in the house of God was vital and anointed, as the eleven Psalms attributed to them (Psalms 42, 44-49, 84, 85, 87, and 88) clearly show.

Psalm 42 contains a well-known passage about one's thirst for God. The sons of Korah write, "As the hart panteth after the water brooks, so panteth my soul after thee, O God. My soul thirsteth for God, for the living God: when shall I come and appear before God?" (Ps. 42:1-2). This positive tone, however, is intermingled with a note of depression later in the Psalm.

The brothers were able to find their way out of the darkness of depression as they sang these words: "Why art thou cast down, O my soul? And why art thou disquieted within me? Hope thou in God: for I shall yet praise him, who is the health of my countenance, and my God" (Ps. 42:11). Yes, the sons of Korah found renewed hope in God.

The next Psalm attributed to the Korah brothers eloquently displays their faith in God. They write, "Through thee will we push down our enemies: through thy name will we tread them under that rise up against us" (Ps. 44:5). This Psalm is an affirmation of complete and unswerving trust in God.

They continue this theme in Psalm 45, where the sons of Korah write, "Your throne, O God, is forever and ever; a scepter of righteousness is the scepter of Your kingdom" (Ps. 45:6, NKJV).

In the next Psalm (Psalm 46), we read these familiar words: "God is our refuge and strength, a very present help in trouble. Therefore we will not fear, even though the earth be removed, and though the mountains be carried into the midst of the sea" (Ps. 46:1-2, NKJV).

Psalm 46 is a glorious song of tribute to Almighty God and a song of triumph as well. The brothers conclude this powerful hymn with these insightful words, "Be still, and know that I am God: I will be exalted among the nations, I will be exalted in the earth" (Ps. 46:10, NKJV). To them, God is all-powerful and fully deserving of all the honor and glory we can give to Him.

The sons of Korah promote a tone of joy and rejoicing in their next Psalm (Psalm 47). They write, "Oh, clap your hands, all you peoples! Shout to God with the voice of triumph! For the Lord Most High is awesome; He is a great King over all the earth" (Ps. 47:1-2, NKJV).

This leads these Psalmists into their next hymn of praise and glory to God. They write, "Great is the Lord, and greatly to be praised in the city of our God, in the mountain of his holiness" (Ps. 48:1).

This magnificent song of praise concludes with these words, "For this God is our God for ever and ever: he will be our guide even unto death" (Ps. 48:14).

Wisdom is the theme of Psalm 49, in which the sons of Korah speak against those who place their trust in riches rather than God. They point to the folly practiced by such people and explain, "Like sheep are they laid in the grave; death shall feed on them; and the upright shall have dominion over them in the morning" (Ps. 49:14).

Despite the seemingly negative tone of Psalm 49, the sons of Korah are careful to paint a vivid contrast between the deaths of the servants of Mammon (money and materialism) and the servants of God.

They write, "But God will redeem my soul from the power of the grave: for he shall receive me. Selah" (Ps. 49:15).

The intimation of eternal life for believers is present in this Psalm, pointing us to the death and resurrection of Christ that led Paul to write, "O death, where is thy sting? O grave, where is thy victory?" (1 Cor. 15:55).

Psalm 84, also written by the Korah brothers, is a very strong and positive tribute to God and the importance of worship and being in His house.

They inspire us with these words, "For the Lord God is a sun and shield: the Lord will give grace and glory; no good thing will he withhold from them that walk uprightly. O Lord of hosts, blessed is the man that trusteth in thee" (Ps. 84:11-12).

The sons of Korah proclaim God's goodness and forgiveness in Psalm 85. They remind us of the following truths: "Lord, You have been favorable to Your land; You have brought back the captivity of Jacob. You have forgiven the iniquity of Your people; You have covered all their sin" (Ps. 85:1-2, NKJV).

In Psalm 87, the emphasis is upon Zion, the city of God, as it was in Psalm 48. The sons of Korah write, "His foundation is in the holy mountains. The Lord loveth the gates of Zion more than all the dwellings of Jacob. Glorious things are spoken of thee, O city of God. Selah" (Ps. 87:1-3).

The last of the Psalms written by the sons of Korah is a prayer to God for help. It is based on the brothers' belief in God's great faithfulness. They write, "O Lord God of my salvation, I have cried day and night before thee: Let my prayer come before thee: incline thine ear unto my cry" (Ps. 88:1-2).

Though we are not privileged to read the answer to their prayer, we can be sure God heard and answered them. Most surely He supplied their need, as He always does in the lives of those who trust Him as the sons of Korah did.

These brothers were men of God who loved their heavenly Father with all their hearts. They trusted Him to meet their needs, to protect them from their enemies, and to lead them through every difficulty, even death. Their example, as expressed in their beautiful hymns, is a firm foundation on which to stand and build a life of faith and prayer.

Solomon

Solomon was considered by many to be the wisest man who ever lived, and the two

Psalms he wrote (Psalms 72 and 127) certainly reflect the God-given wisdom he possessed and so clearly cherished. This great man was the tenth son of David, and his name means "peace" or "peaceable."

Solomon was the third king of Israel, and his reign lasted for forty years. Like his father, David, Solomon was also known as "beloved of the Lord," a translation of another name that was given to him — Jedidiah.

Solomon was a gifted servant of God, who eventually fell into sins related to sexuality and greed.

Alexander Whyte writes of Solomon's downfall: "The shipwreck of Solomon is surely the most terrible tragedy in all the world. For if ever there was a shining type of Christ in the Old Testament church, it was Solomon....but everyday sensuality made him in the end a castaway."

In his earlier years, however, Solomon was a master musician, a great leader, and an excellent writer. In Psalm 72, he writes these words in honor and praise to God: "Blessed be the Lord God, the God of Israel, who only doeth wondrous things. And blessed be his glorious name for ever: and let the whole earth be filled with his glory; Amen, and Amen" (Ps. 72:18-19).

The other Psalm that is attributed to Solomon is Psalm 127, where the great king tells us, "Except the Lord build the house, they labour in vain that build it: except the Lord keep the city, the watchman waketh but in vain" (Ps. 127:1).

He then goes on to advise us, "It is vain for you to rise up early, to sit up late, to eat the bread of sorrows: for so he giveth his beloved sleep" (Ps. 127:2).

Next, Solomon reminds us of the importance of children. He writes, "Lo, children are an heritage of the Lord: and the fruit of the womb is his reward. As arrows are in the hand of a mighty man; so are children of the youth. Happy is the man that hath his quiver full of them: they shall not be ashamed, but they shall speak with the enemies in the gate" (Ps. 127:3-5).

King Solomon was a paradox in many ways, but his Psalms, the Song of Solomon, and the Book of Proverbs reveal that he loved God deeply and recognized that God's glory far exceeded his own in every way.

Moses

Known as "God's friend," Moses was a great leader who committed his life fully to God. To try and condense the life and ministry of Moses into a short biographical sketch is quite impossible, for he was an excellent writer, historian, leader of unparalleled greatness, servant of God, and prophet whom God knew "face to face." (See Deut. 34:10.)

His one Psalm (Psalm 90) tells us a great deal about him and his faith. He writes, "Lord, thou hast been our dwelling place in all generations. Before the mountains were brought forth, or ever thou hadst formed the earth and the world, even from everlasting to everlasting, thou art God" (Ps. 90:1-2).

He goes on, "So teach us to number our days, that we may gain a heart of wisdom....Oh, satisfy us early with Your mercy, that we may rejoice and be glad all our days!...Let Your work appear unto Your servants, and Your glory to their children. And let the beauty of the Lord our God be upon us, and establish the work of our hands for us; yes, establish the work of our hands" (Ps. 90:12-17, NKJV).

Moses had an intimate relationship with God, his heavenly Father. It was to Moses that God gave His commandments and the first five books of the Bible, which are known as the Pentateuch or the Law.

In Moses, we see a type of Christ, a man of God who lived to serve his Lord and lead God's people out of the darkness and drudgery of slavery into a life of freedom and joy in Him.

Ethan

Little is known about Ethan, except for the fact that he was another one of David's appointed song leaders. We read this about him in First Chronicles: "Then David spoke to the leaders of the Levites to appoint their brethren to be the singers accompanied by instruments of music, stringed instruments, harps and cymbals, by raising the voice with resounding joy.

"So the Levites appointed Heman the son of Joel; and of his brethren, Asaph the son of Berechiah; and of their brethren, the sons of Merari, Ethan the son of Kushaiah" (1 Chron. 15:16-17, NKJV).

Psalm 89 is attributed to Ethan. In this stirring Psalm, we find a majestic hymn that beautifully portrays the faithfulness of God to all generations. Ethan writes, "I will sing of the mercies of the Lord for ever: with my mouth will I make known thy faithfulness to all generations" (Ps. 89:1).

Ethan's goal in this Psalm is to let people know that God is absolutely trustworthy in every respect, and he does so by vividly describing the attributes of God, including His mercy, strength, sovereignty, justice, glory, and faithfulness to His covenant with His people.

Ethan concludes these powerful reflections with these words: "Blessed be the Lord for evermore. Amen, and Amen" (Ps. 89:52).

David

In chapter one, we have already cited several of David's Psalms. Therefore, we will not quote many of his works in this chapter. Instead, we will provide a brief synopsis of his life. He is said to be the author of seventy-three Psalms. Often, when the word "Psalmist" is used to describe a writer of the Psalms, it is synonymous with David.

David, whose name means "beloved," was the youngest son of Jesse. He became the second king of Israel. Many believe he was the greatest king of Israel. He also served as a shepherd, a valiant warrior, a musician, an eloquent writer, a poet, and a prophet.

Most people remember David's youthful triumph over the giant Goliath. The young warrior was careful to give the credit for his remarkable victory to God. It appears that David was humble before God as well as obedient.

God raised up David as king, and said of him, "I have found David, the son of Jesse, a man after My own heart, who will do all My will" (Acts 13:22, NKJV). God loved David even though he was a sinner as well as a saint.

David was a gifted harpest, and his music was able to soothe King Saul. His musical abilities are evidenced in the Psalms he wrote, because each one is a masterpiece of rhythm, cadence, artistic prowess, and spiritual life.

David loved God, and his Psalms reflect the preeminence he gave to his heavenly Father. The themes of worship and meditation are paramount in many of his Psalms.

David was a prophet as well. Many of his Psalms are Messianic in nature, pointing to the coming Christ as the Savior of the world.

When David sinned, he experienced great anguish of heart and soul. Some of his Psalms reflect his feelings of guilt and depression that resulted from his sins of plotting murder, living in deceit, and committing adultery.

His painful cries of shame and humiliation help us to relate to his humanity and failure, but in his honest confession of sins, we learn how to break free from our weaknesses and faults. In this, David sets a great example for every believer to follow.

We conclude this chapter by looking at David's prescription for happiness, peace, health, and wholeness as it is reflected in the "beatitudes" he wrote:

"Blessed is he whose transgression is forgiven, whose sin is covered" (Ps. 32:1).

"Blessed is the man unto whom the Lord imputeth not iniquity, and in whose spirit there is no guile" (Ps. 32:2).

"O taste and see that the Lord is good: blessed is the man that trusteth in him" (Ps. 34:8).

"Blessed is he that considereth the poor: the Lord will deliver him in time of trouble. The Lord will preserve him, and keep him alive; and he shall be blessed upon the earth: and thou wilt not deliver him unto the will of his enemies" (Ps. 41:1-2).

Learning to Pray the Psalms

Personalizing the Psalms

Many of the Psalms are written in the form of personal prayers. This, of course, makes them readily adaptable to your own prayer life. (Refer to the final chapter of this book, "Prayers of the Psalmists.")

A good example of this is found in Psalm 43, where we read: "Judge me, O God, and plead my cause....O deliver me from the deceitful and unjust man. For thou art the God of my strength....O send out thy light and thy truth: let them lead me; let them bring me unto thy holy hill, and to thy tabernacles" (Ps. 43:1-3).

As you learn to pray the Psalms as personal prayers from your own heart, you will soon discover that they have great power to help you in every area of your life, because they will lift you up, give you a new perspective, and help you see God and your circumstances as they really are.

Almost every passage in the Scriptures can be prayed to God, but the Psalms are particularly rich and meaningful in this regard, because many of them are styled as personal prayers already. To personalize them, therefore, is simply to pray them as they are written, as if you are the Psalmist who originally wrote them.

As you prepare to pray a specific Psalm, be sure to ask yourself these personalizing questions about the passage:

1. *What does this passage teach me about Jesus Christ?* At first glance this may seem to be an unusual question, because the Psalms were written a millennium or so before the birth of Christ. However, many of the Psalms are Messianic in nature in that they point the reader to the coming Messiah (Jesus Christ) who will one day rule the earth. All of the Old Testament looks forward to God's promised Messiah, for this was the gospel God intended that His chosen people convey to the lost world.

2. *Is there any error in this passage for me to avoid?* The Psalmists, as you know, had feet of clay. Like all of us, they were sinners in need of a Savior. Sometimes they allude to their sins in the Psalms, and when this is so, you need to be careful to avoid the same

sins in your own life and to ask God to keep you from falling.

3. *Is there any command in this passage for me to obey?* The Psalms are filled with directions, statutes, and commandments from God, and these are requirements He has set forth in His wisdom to bless you and protect you. His commandments come always with His promise to help you keep them. For example, the Psalmists frequently exhort you to praise God, to give Him glory, and to worship Him. These express the divine purpose of reminding you of God's greatness and His love. He wants to draw you to reverent obedience and the warm fellowship He knows is your place of blessing. Because God loves you so much, He emphatically calls you to comply with His commandments, and He has given you the Holy Spirit to help you keep them.

4. *Is there any example in this passage for me to follow?* As we pointed out earlier, David frequently humbled himself, prayed, and sought the Lord's forgiveness. This is an excellent example for every believer to follow. Other examples to follow in the Psalms

include correct attitudes, righteous living, prayer, praise, and generosity.

5. *Is there any promise in this passage for me to claim?* God's Word is a book filled with promises for you to claim, receive, and believe. The Psalms provide you with hundreds of personal promises from God for your life. For example, you can claim this truth from Psalm 91, a chapter that is particularly replete with God's promises: "Because thou hast made the Lord, which is my refuge, even the most High, thy habitation; there shall no evil befall thee, neither shall any plague come nigh thy dwelling" (Ps. 91:9-10).

What a wonderful promise this is for you and your family. No evil shall befall you! Praise God.

So, make the Psalms personal. Let their words become the core of your prayers. This will foster an intimate, personal relationship with God, who promises to hear and answer your prayers.

In fact, John writes, "And this is the confidence that we have in him, that, if we ask any thing according to his will, he heareth us: And if we know that he hear us, whatsoever we ask, we know that we have the petitions that we desired of him" (1 John 5:14-15). This is a powerful prayer promise from the Bible, and it is a promise for you to claim.

To pray according to the will of God is to pray according to His Word, for the Bible presents the full counsel of God. If you pray according to His will, as it is revealed in His Word, you can be confident that He hears you.

The Apostle John goes on to declare that, if you know God hears you, you also know He will grant your petitions. This is a wonderful promise of answered prayer; it is one for you to trust as you pray the Psalms.

You will soon discover that most of the Psalms are very personal in nature, and they deal with most of the doctrines and concepts that are important to Christians. This makes them ideal bases for your personal prayer life.

Utilizing God's Word as a Prayer Source

Paul wrote these words to Timothy: "All scripture is given by inspiration of God, and is profitable for doctrine, for reproof, for correction, for instruction in righteousness: that the man of God may be perfect, thoroughly furnished unto all good works" (2 Tim. 3:16-17). God's Word is profitable in your life for so many things, including prayer.

As in all things, the Bible is the light that guides us. The Psalmist wrote, "Thy word is a lamp unto my feet, and a light unto my path" (Ps. 119:105). Let the light of God's Word guide you as you pray the Book of Psalms, for it is an effective manual to use in learning the life of prayer.

By using the Psalms both as the framework and substance for your prayers, you will be praying with confidence, power, authority, wisdom, and direction from God's Word. In fact, you will have God's answers as you pray.

John Bunyan, the author of *Pilgrim's Progress*, wrote, "Prayer is a sincere, sensible, affectionate pouring out of the soul to God through Christ in the strength and assistance of the Spirit, for such things as God has promised."

The things God has promised are found in His Word, and as you pray the Psalms, you will experience the strength of Christ and the power of the Holy Spirit.

As you study the Word of God, you will learn to pray effectually, after God's own heart. In effect, this is what Martin Luther was saying when he wrote, "To pray well is the better half of study."

Paul wrote, "Study to show thyself approved to God, a workman that needeth not to be ashamed, rightly dividing the word of truth" (2 Tim. 2:15).

Praying the Psalms is praying the Word of God, and, as you do so, God will enable you to divide His truth correctly and appropriately. To divide His Word rightly is to handle it in the most appropriate ways possible throughout your life, including your own prayer life.

The well-known missionary, Frank C. Laubach, pointed out, "Prayer at its highest is a two-way conversation, and for me the most important part is listening to God's replies."

Praying the Word of God gives you God's replies as you pray. His thoughts, truths, answers, and desires invade your prayers when you utilize His Word in your prayer life.

Paul wrote, "Let the word of Christ dwell in you richly in all wisdom....And whatsoever ye do in word or deed, do all in the name of the Lord Jesus, giving thanks to God and the Father by him" (Col. 3:16-17).

As the word of Christ dwells in you richly, in all wisdom, it will naturally become a part of your prayer life, and you will, therefore, be able to pray in the name of the Lord Jesus Christ, giving thanks to the Father by Him.

The great prayer warrior and master teacher of prayer, R.A. Torrey, pointed out that the scriptural promises of prayer are based on this: "If we are to receive from God all we ask from Him, Christ's words must abide in us. We must study His words and let them sink into our thoughts and heart. We must keep them in our memory, obey them constantly in our life, and let them shape and mold our daily life and our every act.

"This is really the method of abiding in Christ. It is through His words that Jesus imparts Himself to us. The words He speaks unto us, they are spirit and they are life (John 6:63). It is vain to expect power in prayer unless we meditate upon the words of Christ and let them sink deep and find a permanent abode in our hearts.

"There are many who wonder why they are so powerless in prayer. The very simple explanation of it all is found in their neglect of the words of Christ. They have not hidden His words in their hearts; His words do not abide in them. It is not by moments of mystical meditation and rapturous experiences that we learn to abide in Christ.

"It is by feeding upon His Word, His written word in the Bible, and looking to the Spirit to implant these words in our heart — to thus make them a living thing in our heart. If we thus let the words of Christ abide in us, they will stir us up to prayer. *They will be the mold in which our prayers are shaped.*

"And, our prayers will necessarily be along the line of God's will and will prevail with Him. Prevailing prayer is almost an impossibility where there is neglect of the study of God's Word" (From *How to Pray* by R.A. Torrey).

Therefore, learn to shape your prayers according to the Word of God, including the Book of Psalms. Jesus said, "If you abide in Me, and My words abide in you, you will ask what you desire, and it shall be done for you" (John 15:7, NKJV).

The Lord Jesus Christ also said, "Ask, and it shall be given you; seek, and ye shall find; knock, and it shall be opened unto you" (Matt. 7:7). Faith that God will answer your prayers is cultivated by adhering to biblical principles that will never fail.

One of these infallible principles involves praying according to the will of God, as it is revealed in His Word.

Doing so will bring into your life everything God wants for you. E.M. Bounds, a well-known author on prayer, wrote, "To know God's will in prayer, we must be filled with God's Spirit, who makes intercession for the saints according to the will of God. To be filled with God's Spirit, to be filled with God's Word, is to know God's will. It is to be put in such a frame of mind and state of heart that it will enable us to read and correctly interpret the purposes of the infinite.

"Such filling of the heart with the Word and the Spirit gives us an insight into the will of the Father. It enables us to rightly discern His will and puts a disposition of mind and heart within us to make it the guide and compass of our lives" (From *The Necessity of Prayer* by E.M. Bounds).

Familiarity with God's Word and praying from its perspective always produce profound and phenomenal changes both in your praying and your living. In fact, these approaches will affect all that you say, think, pray, and do, because this style of praying unleashes the power of God, through the Holy Spirit, into your life.

As you learn to pray the Psalms, you will learn how to accept the will of God, even if you discover that His will is different from what you may have originally hoped. David wrote, "Thy word have I hid in mine heart, that I might not sin against thee" (Ps. 119:11).

When God's Word finds its rightful abode within your heart, your will becomes more in tune with the Father's will. There is no longer any strain or tension about it, because you have learned to accept His will as your own.

As you conform your will to the Father's will (through the operation of His Word and His Spirit in your life), you will know and believe that your prayers will be answered.

Paul wrote, "And be not conformed to this world: but be ye transformed by the renewing of your mind, that ye may prove what is that good, and acceptable, and perfect, will of God" (Rom. 12:2). God's Word enables you to renew your mind.

The Worth of the Psalms

The Book of Psalms has been a valuable prayer book used by Jews and Christians throughout the centuries. Jesus himself often quoted from the Psalms, and, in the final moments of His life, He prayed from the Psalms, as well. (See Matt. 27:46, and Luke 23:46.)

What is the inherent value of the Psalms? For one thing, they teach us what God is like by revealing to us His attributes, in all their glory, to us. They show how much God wants to have an intimate relationship with His children and how much He cares about each one of us.

The Psalms declare His great mercy and love for us. The Psalmists also show God as the omnipresent One, "...a very present help in trouble" (Ps. 46:1).

In the Psalms, we learn about the coming Christ, the One who saves believers from sin and death. Jesus alluded to this fact when He said, "These are the words which I spake unto you, while I was yet with you, that all things must be fulfilled, which were written in the law of Moses, and in the prophets, and in the psalms, concerning me" (Luke 24:44).

The Psalms are filled with warnings against sin in all its hideous forms, including idolatry, lust, materialism, robbery, unfairness, murder, violence, terrorism, and disobedience. They help us to see the importance of confession and repentance as antidotes to the effects of darkness and evil in our lives.

The Psalms have a lot to teach us about nature, as well, by vividly describing the glorious beauty of God's creation. In addition, they teach us about human nature and the motives that drive people either to or away from God.

Manna for the Church

Jesus loved the Psalms, and He prayed them as well. As He was dying on the cross, He cried, "Eli, Eli, lama sabachthani" (Matt. 27:46). This comes directly from Psalm 22:1:

"My God, my God, why hast thou forsaken me?"

Soon thereafter, the Son of God prayed, "Father, into thy hands I commend my spirit" (Luke 23:46). His final prayer was based on Psalm 31:5: "Into thine hand I commit my spirit: thou hast redeemed me, O Lord God of truth."

Throughout church history, men and women have turned to the Psalter for strength, inspiration, comfort, and direction. One of these was Dietrich Bonhoeffer, a Lutheran pastor who was imprisoned for his stand against Hitler and Nazism during the Third Reich.

Bonhoeffer called the Psalms, "...a great school of prayer," and his last published work revealed his deep appreciation for this central book of the Bible; it was entitled, *Psalms: the Prayer Book of the Bible*.

Likewise, Martin Luther loved the Psalms. He preached from the Psalms frequently and translated them into a very rhythmic style of poetry. He turned many of the Psalms into hymns as well.

Johann Sebastian Bach composed many of his chorales from Luther's translation of the Psalms. Bach's ability to blend musical beauty with scriptural truth remains unsurpassed to this day.

It is reported that many priests and monks during the Middle Ages knew the Psalms by heart, and sometimes this memorization of the Psalms was a prerequisite to priestly ordination. Surely, Saint Francis of Assisi was well acquainted with the Psalms, for his "Canticle of Brother Sun" is based upon Psalm 148.

Thomas a Kempis, the author of *The Imitation of Christ*, was greatly influenced by the Psalms in his devotional writing. In fact, his model for Book III of that great work came from the Psalms: "I will hearken to what the Lord God will say concerning me; for he shall speak peace unto his people and to his saints that they turn not again to folly" (based on Ps. 85:8).

Christian martyrs have frequently found great solace in the Psalms. For example, John Huss, the Bohemian Protestant reformer, quoted Psalm 31 as he went to the stake.

Imagine the impact of these words of the condemned Huss on those who heard him: "In thee, O Lord, do I put my trust; let me never be ashamed: deliver me in thy righteousness.

"Bow down thine ear to me; deliver me speedily: be thou my strong rock, for an house of defence to save me. For thou art my rock and my fortress; therefore for thy name's sake lead me, and guide me.

"Pull me out of the net that they have laid privily for me: for thou art my strength. Into thine hand I commit my spirit: thou hast redeemed me, O Lord God of truth" (Ps. 31:1-5).

A year later, Jerome of Prague recited these same words as he was being executed for his faith. Within the same century, Savonarola, an Italian reformer, while he lay dying in a dungeon, after severe torture that left him with only one hand, wrote a stirring meditation on Psalms 31 and 41.

Sir Thomas More, boyhood friend and long-time advisor to King Henry VIII, repeated Psalm 51:1 as he awaited his execution for refusing to honor the king as God's sole representative on earth.

This verse from the Psalms was More's final prayer: "Have mercy upon me, O God, according to thy lovingkindness: according unto the multitude of thy tender mercies blot out my transgressions" (Ps. 51:1).

Many Christian martyrs, Protestants who were hunted throughout Europe for more than a century, often went to the stake or the gallows singing, "This is the day which the Lord hath made; we will rejoice and be glad in it" (Ps. 118:24).

The Puritans who bravely sailed across the Atlantic, seeking religious freedom, often sang the Psalms on board their ships. They chose a name for their first settlement in Massachusetts from Psalm 76: "In Judah is God known: his name is great in Israel. In Salem also is his tabernacle, and his dwelling place in Zion" (Ps. 76:1-2). Salem, Massachusetts, remains a well-known town in New England.

In 1787, at the Constitutional Convention that convened in Philadelphia, Pennsylvania, the framers of the Constitution of the United States reminded each other of this verse from the Psalter: "Except the Lord build the house, they labour in vain that build it" (Ps. 127:1).

Throughout the centuries, the Psalms have been central to the life and thought of God's people. For this reason, John Donne, a seventeenth-century poet and preacher, wrote, "The Psalms are the manna of the church."

Yes, the Psalms are manna, spiritual food provided by God to give believers great strength, hope, comfort, and truth. For this reason, and many others, it is appropriate to pray the Psalms on a daily basis. The next sections of this book will guide you into this dynamic and life-changing experience.

Bible-Based Prayers

The next three chapters of this book provide you with Bible-based prayers from the Book of Psalms.

In chapter five, you will discover topical prayers that were adapted and built from verses of various Psalms woven together. In so doing, we have been careful to footnote every Bible passage used and to list the references at the end of each prayer.

Then, in chapter six, we have selected certain significant Psalms to use as our Psalter of personal prayer. The particular Psalms we've selected have been adapted and paraphrased as dynamic personal prayers for your own use.

Finally, in chapter seven, we have written paraphrases that we have adapted from actual prayers that were written by the Psalmists. You will find these to be richly rewarding prayers to use in your own devotional life.

May the God of the Psalms lead you, guide you, inspire you, meet you, and supply all your needs, as you pray His Word.

Topical

Prayers

The following prayers are built directly from the Psalms. They are personal prayers for you to use regarding specific issues and topics that are important to you. These Psalm-prayers are alphabetically arranged to make them easy to find, and, every time a biblical reference is used, it's footnoted and listed at the end of the prayer.

Each prayer is composed from related verses of different Psalms blended together in coherent ways. This approach to prayer is one that will fortify your faith, strengthen your hope, and increase your love for God and others. You will be amazed to see how your confidence in God will grow, as you pray and meditate on these prayers.

God will be magnified, and you will be blessed as you use these prayers in your own devotions and quiet times with the Father.

1

Adoration of God

Prayer Purpose: To express adoration to your heavenly Father.

Key Scripture: *"Great is the Lord, and greatly to be praised in the city of our God, in the mountain of his holiness. Beautiful for situation, the joy of the whole earth, is mount Zion, on the sides of the north, the city of the great King"* (Ps. 48:1-2).

Prayer: O God, my Father, you are incomparably great, and you are greatly to be praised.[1] I do, indeed, praise you with all my heart, and I adore you with all that is within me.

You, O Lord God, shall endure forever, and all generations shall remember you.[2] You are my refuge and my strength, a very present help to me in time of trouble.[3] Thank you, Father.

You are Almighty God, and I adore you. It thrills me to know that you spoke and called forth the earth from the rising of the sun to the going down of the same.[4] Out of Zion, the perfection of beauty, you have shined.[5]

O God, you are my God. Early will I seek you, because my soul thirsts for you. I adore you in all your power and glory, Father.[6] Because your lovingkindness is better than life to me, my lips shall praise you and I will bless you while I live. I will lift up my hands in your name, dear God.[7]

Father, I thank you that you are the King who reigns over all your creation. You are clothed with majesty and strength. You have established the earth in such a way that it shall not be moved. Your throne is established from old, and you are from everlasting.[8] Thank you, God.

Blessed are you, O Father, for you are my strength. You teach my hands to war and my fingers to fight. You are my goodness, my fortress, my high tower, and my Deliverer.

Father, you are my shield, and I trust completely in you.[9] Thank you, dear God. I will extol you, mighty God, and I will bless your name forever.

Every day I will bless you, and I will praise your name forever and ever, for you are truly great and your greatness is unsearchable.[10]

Father God, you shall reign forever unto all generations.[11] I love you and adore you with all my heart. In Jesus' name I pray, Amen.[12]

References: (1) Psalm 48:1-2; (2) Psalm 102:12; (3) Psalm 46:1; (4) Psalm 50:1; (5) Psalm 50:2; (6) Psalm 63:1-2; (7) Psalm 63:3-4; (8) Psalm 93:1-2; (9) Psalm 144:1-2; (10) Psalm 145:1-3; (11) Psalm 146:10; (12) John 16:23.

2

Angelic Protection

Prayer Purpose: To express faith to God that His angels will protect you.

Key Scripture: *"No evil shall befall you, nor shall any plague come near your dwelling. For He shall give his angels charge over you, to keep you in all your ways. In their hands they shall bear you up, lest you dash your foot against a stone"* (Ps. 91:10-12, NKJV).

Prayer: Mighty Father, my King and my God, thank you for the promises of angelic protection you have given to me in your glorious Word.

I express my faith to you that no evil will befall me, because I know you have given your angels charge over me, to keep me and protect me. I truly believe they will bear me up in their hands and keep me from harm.[1] Thank you, Father.

It is such a blessing to know that your angels encamp around me and deliver me.[2] This brings great joy and confidence to me, Lord God. I ask you to let your angels protect me at all times and defend me from the enemy and all enemies that threaten me. Let them be as chaff before the wind, and let your angels chase them, Father.[3]

Your chariots and angels, dear God, are numbered in the thousands of thousands, and you are among them.[4] You have ascended on high and led captivity captive.[5] You have given me so much.

Blessed are you, my Father, for you daily load me with benefits, and you are the God of my salvation.[6] Thank you for the wonderful benefit of angelic protection I enjoy on a daily basis, both today and every day.

My soul blesses you, O God, for you are very great. In fact, you are clothed with honor and majesty.[7] You cover yourself with light as with a garment, and you stretch out the heavens like a curtain.[8]

You lay the beams of your chambers in the waters, and you make the clouds your chariot. You walk upon the wings of the wind.[9] Thank you, dear God, for making your angels to be spirits and a flaming fire.[10] Let them minister everywhere by your great power.

Therefore, Father, for all of these reasons, and for the assurance of angelic protection you give to me, I join with the company of angels in heaven who are praising you forever. I praise you, almighty God, for you commanded and all creation came to be.[11] In the wondrous name of your Son, Jesus Christ, I pray, Amen.[12]

References: (1) Psalm 91:10-12; (2) Psalm 34:7; (3) Psalm 35:5-6; (4) Psalm 68:17; (5) Psalm 68:18; (6) Psalm 68:19; (7) Psalm 104:1; (8) Psalm 104:2; (9) Psalm 104:3; (10) Psalm 104:4; (11) Psalm 148:1-5; (12) John 15:16.

3

Believing God

Prayer Purpose: To build your faith in God and His Word.

Key Scripture: *"I had fainted, unless I had believed to see the goodness of the Lord in the land of the living. Wait on the Lord: be of good courage, and he shall strengthen thine heart: wait, I say, on the Lord"* (Ps. 27:13-14).

Prayer: Dear Father, I believe your Word, and I believe in your goodness. Therefore, I wait on you in faith. Help me to be of good courage, and strengthen my heart, as I wait on you.[1] Thank you, Father, for hearing and answering my prayer. I believe in you with all my heart.

Because I know all the wondrous works you have done for me and others, I believe your words, that they are promises to me and for me.[2] Gracious, righteous, and merciful are you, O God.[3]

Thank you for preserving the simple and for helping me.[4] My soul returns to its rest, because you have dealt so bountifully with me.[5] Thank you, Father.

You have delivered my soul from death, my eyes from tears, and my feet from falling.[6] For all these reasons, and many more, I will walk before you in the land of the living, and I will believe in you with all my soul.[7] Because I believe in you, help me to speak forth in your behalf at every possible opportunity.[8]

Thank you for always dealing well with me according to your Word, dear Father.[9] Teach me good judgment and knowledge, for I believe all your words and your commandments.[10]

Dear God, you are good and you always do good. Therefore, I ask you to teach me your statutes.[11]

Father, you are my comfort,[12] my strength,[13] and my protection.[14] Thank you for leading me to believe in you and your Word. Help me to build my faith at all times. In the matchless name of Jesus I pray, Amen.[15]

References: (1) Psalm 27:13-14; (2) Psalm 106:7-12; (3) Psalm 116:5; (4) Psalm 116:6; (5) Psalm 116:7; (6) Psalm 116:8; (7) Psalm 116:9; (8) Psalm 116:10; (9) Psalm 119:65; (10) Psalm 119:66; (11) Psalm 119:68; (12) Psalm 23:4; (13) Psalm 27:1; (14) Psalm 35; (15) John 16:24.

4

Blessing God

Prayer Purpose: To bless and praise God for all the good things He has done for you.

Key Scripture: *"I will bless the Lord at all times: his praise shall continually be in my mouth. My soul shall make her boast in the Lord: the humble shall hear thereof, and be glad"* (Ps. 34:1-3).

Prayer: Lord God, I will bless you at all times. Your praise shall continually be in my mouth. My soul shall make its boast in you, and the humble shall hear thereof and be glad.[1]

In fact, I command my soul to bless you, Father, and all that is within me shall bless your holy name.[2] I will bless you and never forget all your wonderful benefits to me.[3] Thank you, Father.

I praise you for forgiving all my iniquities and healing all my diseases.[4] Thank you, as well, for redeeming my life from destruction, and crowning me with your lovingkindness and tender mercies.[5]

You always satisfy my mouth with good things, so my youth is renewed like the eagle's.[6] Thank you, mighty God.

I bless you, dear Father, for you are incomparably great. Indeed, you are clothed with honor and majesty.[7] I extol you, O God, my King, and I will bless your name forever.[8]

Every day I will bless you, and I will praise you forever.[9] You are so great and greatly to be praised; truly your greatness is unsearchable.[10]

It is so good and pleasant to bless you and sing praises to you, dear Father.[11] Thank you for healing my broken heart and binding up all my wounds.[12]

Therefore, I sing unto you with thanksgiving and I sing praise unto you, O God.[13] Blessing you brings me wonderful joy. In the beautiful name of Jesus Christ, I bless you, Father God, Amen.[14]

References: (1) Psalm 34:1-3; (2) Psalm 103:1; (3) Psalm 103:2; (4) Psalm 103:3; (5) Psalm 103:4; (6) Psalm 103:5; (7) Psalm 104:1; (8) Psalm 145:1; (9) Psalm 145:2; (10) Psalm 145:3; (11) Psalm 147:1; (12) Psalm 147:3; (13) Psalm 147:7; (14) John 15:16.

5

Blessings

Prayer Purpose: To reflect on all the blessings God has bestowed upon you, and to thank Him for His goodness to you.

Key Scripture: *"Bless the Lord, O my soul, and forget not all his benefits: Who forgives all your iniquities, who heals all your diseases, who redeems your life from destruction, who crowns you with lovingkindness and tender mercies, who satisfies your mouth with good things, so that your youth is renewed like the eagle's"* (Ps. 103:2-5, NKJV).

Prayer: O Lord God, my soul blesses you as I contemplate all your wonderful blessings in my life. Thank you, Father, for forgiving all my iniquities, healing all my diseases, redeeming my life from destruction, crowning me with your tender lovingkindness and mercy, satisfying my mouth with good things, and renewing my youth.[1] Blessed be your name, Lord God.

Thank you for the blessings of your goodness in my life.[2] How I praise you that your blessing is upon your people, Father, and I thank you that I am one of your people.[3] You are my shield and my glory. You are the one who lifts up my head.[4] I receive blessing and righteousness from you, Lord, for you are the God of my salvation.[5]

Lord God, you are my Shepherd. Therefore, I shall never suffer want.[6] You make me lie down in green pastures, and you lead me beside the still waters.[7]

Thank you for restoring my soul and leading me in the paths of righteousness for your name's sake.[8] Because you are with me, I will fear no evil.[9] Your rod and staff bring me great comfort.[10]

You have even prepared a table before me in the presence of my enemies. Thank you for doing so and for anointing my head with oil.[11]

Because of your blessings in my life, dear Father, my cup overflows.[12] Thank you so much for being a God who loves to bless His children. I rejoice to realize how much you love me and have blessed me.

Surely goodness and mercy shall follow me all the days of my life, and I shall dwell in your house forever.[13] Hallelujah! I am so wonderfully blessed. In Jesus' matchless name I pray, Amen.[14]

References: (1) Psalm 103:2-5; (2) Psalm 21:3; (3) Psalm 3:8; (4) Psalm 3:3; (5) Psalm 24:5; (6) Psalm 23:1; (7) Psalm 23:2; (8) Psalm 23:3; (9) Psalm 23:4; (10) Psalm 23:4; (11) Psalm 23:5; (12) Psalm 23:5; (13) Psalm 23:6; (14) John 16:24.

6

Children

Prayer Purpose: A prayer to be used by parents, to thank God for your children, and to ask Him to bless them.

Key Scripture: *"Lo, children are an heritage of the Lord: and the fruit of the womb is his reward"* (Ps. 127:3).

Prayer: Father God, thank you for my children. I realize they are an inheritance I have freely received from your hands. Thank you so much for rewarding me with such wonderful children.[1] My children are like arrows in the hands of a mighty man.[2] Thank you, Father.

Thank you, also, for the great happiness my children bring to me. I claim your promise, Father, in their behalf, that they shall not be put to shame throughout their lives.[3]

Indeed, I thank you that you make my children flourish like olive plants round about my table.[4] Thank you, Father, for your promise that I shall see my grandchildren and experience your peace.[5] I believe and accept all the promises of your Word.

Help my children to keep your covenant and testimony at all times, dear Father.[6] Show them the power of your Word, dear God, and the importance of hiding your Word in their hearts, so they will not sin against you.[7] Thank you for strengthening the bars of my gates and blessing my children so richly.[8]

Let my children ever be joyful in you, dear Lord God.[9] It is my prayer that you will always take pleasure in them and that you will beautify them with your salvation.[10]

In the mighty name of Jesus I pray, Amen.[11]

References: (1) Psalm 127:3; (2) Psalm 127:4; (3) Psalm 127:5; (4) Psalm 128:3; (5) Psalm 128:6; (6) Psalm 132:12; (7) Psalm 119:11; (8) Psalm 147:13; (9) Psalm 149:2; (10) Psalm 149:4; (11) John 15:23-24.

7

Comfort

Prayer Purpose: To find God's comfort in your time of need.

Key Scripture: *"Yea, though I walk through the valley of the shadow of death, I will fear no evil: for thou art with me; thy rod and thy staff they comfort me"* (Ps. 23:4).

Prayer: Heavenly Father, thank you for your presence in my life. Truly, your rod and staff bring me great comfort, even when I have to walk through the valley of the shadow of death.[1] I rejoice to know that you are always with me,[2] and I ask for your comforting presence to surround me and fill me right now.

Thank you for your promise to comfort me on every side.[3] I will praise you, dear Father, and my lips shall greatly rejoice when I sing unto you.[4] Your Word has given me life, dear God, and it always provides great comfort for me.[5] Thank you so much.

Your merciful kindness in my life gives me wonderful comfort, dear Father.[6] Let your tender mercies come to me, for your law is my delight.[7]

Help me to fix my heart firmly on your Word, that I would never be ashamed.[8] I hope in your Word at all times, Father, and as I do so, I experience your wonderfully comforting presence in my life.[9]

Thank you for being my source of comfort, dear Father, and for imparting your life and lovingkindness to me, that I would ever keep your Word.[10] In the comforting name of Jesus I pray, Amen.[11]

References: (1) Psalm 23:4; (2) Psalm 23:4; (3) Psalm 71:21; (4) Psalm 71:23; (5) Psalm 119:50; (6) Psalm 119:76; (7) Psalm 119:77; (8) Psalm 119:80; (9) Psalm 119:81; (10) Psalm 119:88; (11) John 15:16.

8
Commitment

Prayer Purpose: To commit (or recommit) your life to God and His ways.

Key Scripture: *"Trust in the Lord, and do good; so shalt thou dwell in the land, and verily thou shalt be fed. Delight thyself also in the Lord; and he shall give thee the desires of thine heart. Commit thy way unto the Lord; trust also in him; and he shall bring it to pass. And he shall bring forth thy righteousness as the light, and thy judgment as the noonday"* (Ps. 37:3-6).

Prayer: Almighty God, my heavenly Father, I commit my life to you. I choose to trust you with everything that pertains to me. I thank you for your promise that, as I delight myself in you, you will give me the desires of my heart. I ask you to so work in my life that all my desires will be conformed to your will.[1]

Father, I commit my way to you and I completely trust in you. Therefore, I know you will hear and answer my prayers.[2] Thank you, dear God.

I believe and receive your promise that you shall bring forth righteousness in me as the light and your judgment in my life as the noonday.[3] Thank you, Father. As I commit my life to you, I will rest in you and wait patiently for you.[4]

Lord God, you are my refuge and my strength, a very present help to me in times of trouble.[5] Thank you for helping me in so many ways.

Because of your abiding presence, the many promises of your Word, and the strength you impart to me, I will not fear.[6] Instead, with your help, I will be still and contemplate the fact that you are the eternal God of the universe and of my life as well.[7]

Truly, my soul waits upon you, O God, for you are my Rock and my salvation. You are my defense, and because this is true, I shall not be moved.[8] Thank you for making it possible for me to commit my life to you and to trust you with all my heart.

Help me to trust in you at all times, dear Father. As I pour out my heart before you, I realize you are my refuge.[9] Thank you for meeting all my needs.

O God, you are my God. I will seek you early, because my soul thirsts for you.[10] Indeed, your lovingkindness is better than life to me. Therefore, I will bless you throughout my life.[11]

I give my life to you without any reservation whatsoever, dear God. Keep me and use me as you see fit. In the mighty name of Jesus Christ, my Savior, I pray, Amen.[12]

References: (1) Psalm 37:3-4; (2) Psalm 37:5; (3) Psalm 37:6; (4) Psalm 37:7; (5) Psalm 46:1; (6) Psalm 46:2; (7) Psalm 46:10; (8) Psalm 62:1-2; (9) Psalm 62:8; (10) Psalm 63:1; (11) Psalm 63:3-4; (12) John 15:16.

9

Confession of Sin

Prayer Purpose: To confess your sins to God and receive His forgiveness and cleansing.

Key Scripture: *"Have mercy upon me, O God, according to Your lovingkindness; according to the multitude of Your tender mercies, blot out my transgressions. Wash me thoroughly from my iniquity, and cleanse me from my sin. For I acknowledge my transgressions, and my sin is always before me"* (Ps. 51:1-3, NKJV).

Prayer: O God, have mercy upon me according to your lovingkindness. Thank you for your tender mercies toward me, which lead you to blot out my transgressions.

Wash me thoroughly from my iniquity and cleanse me from my sins, for I acknowledge my sins to you, Father. Indeed, I confess the following sins to you now: [1]_____

_____

_____.

It grieves me to realize that I have sinned against you, dear God, and to know that I've done evil in your sight.[2] Indeed, I was conceived in sin and formed in iniquity.[3]

Purge me, Father, and I shall be clean.[4] Because I know you desire truth in my inner being, I ask you to impart your wisdom to me and fill me with your truth.[5]

Cause me to hear joy and gladness once again.[6] Hide your face from my sins, and blot out all my iniquities.[7] Create in me a clean heart, O God, and renew a right spirit within me.[8] Keep me always in your presence, dear Father.[9]

Thank you for hearing and answering my prayer. Restore unto me the joy of your salvation and uphold me with your Spirit.[10] Help me to teach your ways to transgressors, so sinners will be converted to you.[11]

Deliver me, O God of my salvation, and my tongue shall ever sing of your righteousness.[12] Open my lips, dear God, and my mouth will utter your praises.[13] Thank you so much for forgiving me and cleansing me of all my sins.

In the powerful name of Jesus I pray, Amen.[14]

References: (1) Psalm 51:1-3; (2) Psalm 51:4; (3) Psalm 51:5; (4) Psalm 51:7; (5) Psalm 51:6; (6) Psalm 51:8; (7) Psalm 51:9; (8) Psalm 51:10; (9) Psalm 51:11; (10) Psalm 51:12; (11) Psalm 51:13; (12) Psalm 51:14; (13) Psalm 51:15; (14) John 16:23-24.

10

Confidence in God

Prayer Purpose: To ask God to help you build your faith and confidence in Him and to express your confidence in Him.

Key Scripture: *"Though an host should encamp against me, my heart shall not fear: though war should rise against me, in this will I be confident. One thing have I desired of the Lord, that will I seek after; that I may dwell in the house of the Lord all the days of my life, to behold the beauty of the Lord, and to inquire in his temple. For in the time of trouble he shall hide me in his pavilion: in the secret of his tabernacle shall he hide me; he shall set me up upon a rock"* (Ps. 27:3-5).

Prayer: O God, my mighty Father, you are my light and my salvation. Whom shall I fear? You are the strength of my life. Of whom shall I be afraid?[1] I place all my confidence and trust in you, dear God, and I shall not fear, no matter what may come my way.

I will continue to seek after one primary thing, and that is to dwell in your house all the days of my life, to behold your beauty, and to inquire of you in your temple.[2] Thank you, Father, for all the promises of your Word.

Thank you for your promise to hear and answer my prayer, O God, for you are my confidence and the confidence of the whole earth.[3] I need your confidence in my life right now. Thank you for being on my side, dear Father. Because this is true, I will remain confident and never fear what others may try to do to me.[4]

How much better it is to place all my trust in you rather than to place my confidence in others.[5] I trust you, dear God, and I am completely confident in you.

In stillness, I meditate upon you and I stand in awe before you, Father.[6] Help me to trust in you at all times.[7] Thank you for filling my heart with gladness.[8]

Because you have enabled me to place all my confidence in you, I will lie down in peace and sleep restfully. Thank you, Lord God, for allowing me to live safely, free from fear, and fully confident in you.[9]

O Lord, my God, in you do I put my trust.[10] I am confident in you. I love you, O Lord, my strength. You are my Rock, my fortress, my Deliverer, my God, my buckler, my salvation, and my high tower.[11]

As for you, dear Father, I know your way is perfect and your Word is tried and true. Thank you for girding me with strength and confidence and making my way perfect in you.[12]

In Jesus' most precious name I pray, Amen.[13]

References: *(1) Psalm 27:1; (2) Psalm 27:3-5; (3) Psalm 65:5; (4) Psalm 118:6; (5) Psalm 118:8; (6) Psalm 4:4; (7) Psalm 4:5; (8) Psalm 4:7; (9) Psalm 4:8; (10) Psalm 7:1; (11) Psalm 18:1-2; (12) Psalm 18:30-32; (13) John 16:23.*

11

Courage

Prayer Purpose: To ask God for the courage you need to face the circumstances of your life.

Key Scripture: *"Be of good courage, and He shall strengthen your heart, all you who hope in the Lord"* (Ps. 31:24, NKJV).

Prayer: Lord God, I look to you today for the courage I need to face the circumstances of my life. With your help I will be of good courage, and I know you will strengthen my heart, as I place my hope in you.[1] Thank you, Father.

You are my light and my salvation, dear God. Indeed, you are the strength of my life. Therefore, I shall not fear at all.[2] Instead, I will wait on you and be of good courage. Thank you for your promise to strengthen my heart and to help me to be courageous.[3]

Teach me your way, dear God, and lead me in a plain path.[4] I place all my trust in you, Father God. Don't ever let me be ashamed. Deliver me in your righteousness.[5] Hear my prayer, for you are my strong Rock and my fortress.[6] Knowing you answer my prayers gives me courage, Father. Please lead me and guide me at all times.[7]

I will bless you at all times, dear God, and your praise shall continually be in my mouth.[8]

My soul shall make its boast in you, Father, for I have sought you and you have delivered me from all my fears.[9] Thank you for the courage you are imparting to me as I pray.

I have waited patiently for you, O God, and you have heard my cry.[10] Thank you for bringing me out of a horrible pit, setting my feet upon a rock, and establishing my direction and my course.[11]

I praise you for putting a new song into my mouth. It is a song of courage and of strength, because you are my trust.[12] Thank you for meeting my needs, dear God.

In the incomparable name of Jesus I pray, Amen.[13]

References: *(1) Psalm 31:24; (2) Psalm 27:1; (3) Psalm 27:14; (4) Psalm 27:11; (5) Psalm 31:1; (6) Psalm 31:2; (7) Psalm 31:3; (8) Psalm 34:1; (9) Psalm 34:3-4; (10) Psalm 40:1; (11) Psalm 40:2; (12) Psalm 40:3; (13) John 15:16.*

12
Deliverance

Prayer Purpose: To find deliverance from evil and all works of darkness.

Key Scripture: *"In you, O Lord, I put my trust; let me never be put to shame. Deliver me in Your righteousness, and cause me to escape; incline Your ear unto me, and save me. Be my strong refuge, to which I may resort continually; You have given the commandment to save me; for You are my rock and my fortress"* (Ps. 71:1-3, NKJV).

Prayer: In you, O Lord God, do I put my trust. Let me never be put to confusion or shame.[1] Deliver me from _____ in your righteousness, and cause me to escape.

Incline your ear to me and save me.[2] Be my strong habitation unto which I may continually come. Thank you for giving your commandment to save me and deliver me. You, Father, are my Rock and my fortress.[3]

Deliver me, O God, from all evil and from the hand of all evildoers, for you are my hope and my trust.[4] Do not withhold your tender mercies from me, Father.

Let your lovingkindness and truth continually preserve me.[5] Be pleased to deliver me, mighty God, and bring help to me quickly.[6]

Thank you, Father, for all your promises of deliverance, which I find in your glorious Word.[7] As I call upon you in the day of trouble, I claim your promise of complete deliverance.[8] Thank you for hearing and answering my prayer.

O God, in the multitude of your mercy and in the truth of your salvation, hear me.[9] Deliver me out of the mire of these present circumstances, and do not let me sink.[10]

Hear me, O God, for your lovingkindness is so good. Turn unto me according to the multitude of your tender mercies.[11]

I praise you and thank you, dear Father, that you will not hide your face from me when I am in trouble. Thank you for hearing me speedily.[12]

Draw near to my soul and deliver me from all enemies.[13] In Jesus' name I pray, Amen.[14]

References: (1) Psalm 71:1; (2) Psalm 71:2; (3) Psalm 71:3; (4) Psalm 71:4-5; (5) Psalm 40:11; (6) Psalm 40:13; (7) Psalm 50:14; (8) Psalm 50:15; (9) Psalm 69:13; (10) Psalm 69:14; (11) Psalm 69:16; (12) Psalm 69:17; (13) Psalm 69:18; (14) John 15:16.

13

Depression

Prayer Purpose: To seek God's help in overcoming depression in your life.

Key Scripture: *"For You will light my lamp; the Lord my God will enlighten my darkness. For by You I can run against a troop, by my God I can leap over a wall. As for God, His way is perfect; the word of the Lord is proven; He is a shield to all who trust in Him"* (Ps. 18:28-30, NKJV).

Prayer: O God, my God, I believe you will light my candle and bring light to the darkness and depression I have been experiencing.[1] Thank you for this precious promise from your Word.

I believe your way is perfect and your Word is tried and true. Thank you for being a mighty buckler to me, dear Father.[2] I place all my trust in you.[3]

I love you, dear Lord God, my strength.[4] You are my Rock, my fortress, my Deliverer, my God, my strength, my buckler, the horn of my salvation, and my high tower.[5]

Thank you, Father. I call unto you, because I know you are worthy to be praised. In this way I know you will save me from all enemies, including depression and all its causes.[6]

In my distress I call to you, dear God.[7] In you I hope and I know you are hearing me as I pray.[8] Thank you for hearing and answering my prayer and for your promise to deliver me from all depression.[9]

I believe you are bringing me into a far better situation than I have been enduring, because I know you take delight in me.[10] Thank you, Father.

Reward me according to your righteousness.[11] How I thank you that you are girding me with strength and making my way perfect.[12] Thank you for showing me the way out of depression and for commanding your lovingkindness in my life, dear God.[13]

In light of all your promises to me, I realize I have little reason to be cast down, discouraged, depressed, or disquieted, Father, for you are the health of my countenance and my God. I will ever praise you.[14]

In the strong name of Jesus I pray, Amen.[15]

References: (1) Psalm 18:28; (2) Psalm 18:30; (3) Psalm 18:30; (4) Psalm 18:1; (5) Psalm 18:2; (6) Psalm 18:3; (7) Psalm 18:6; (8) Psalm 38:15; (9) Psalm 18:17; (10) Psalm 18:19; (11) Psalm 18:24; (12) Psalm 18:32; (13) Psalm 42:8; (14) Psalm 43:5; (15) John 16:23.

14

Desires of Your Heart

Prayer Purpose: To express your desires to God and to ask Him to fulfill them.

Key Scripture: *"Trust in the Lord, and do good: so shalt thou dwell in the land, and verily thou shalt be fed. Delight thyself also in the Lord; and he shall give thee the desires of thine heart. Commit thy way unto the Lord; trust also in him; and he shall bring it to pass"* (Ps. 37:3-5).

Prayer: O Lord God, my heavenly Father, help me to trust in you and do good. I delight myself in you. Thank you for your promise to give me the desires of my heart as I do so.[1]

Father, I want my desires to be pleasing to you. Therefore, I ask you to keep me from all presumptuous sins and desires.[2] Let the words of my mouth and the meditation of my heart be acceptable in your sight, O Lord God, my strength and my Redeemer.[3]

As I commit my way unto you and trust totally in you, dear God, I believe you will bring my heart's desires to pass.[4] Thank you, Father.

You are King forever, O God, and you know the desires of my heart.[5] Thank you for the assurance your Word gives me, that you will both hear my prayer and grant my heart's desires.[6]

Lord God, all my desires are before you.[7] In you I hope and I know you will hear my prayers.[8] Thank you, Father.

You, dear God, have held me up with your right hand,[9] and you are guiding me with your counsel.[10] Who have I in heaven but you, O God?

I desire you more than anyone or anything.[11] Indeed, you are the strength of my heart, my portion and inheritance forever.[12]

I know you are near to me as I call upon you, Father,[13] and you are fulfilling the desires of my heart as I pray.[14] Thank you for hearing my prayer and granting my heart's desires.[15]

In Jesus' name I pray, Amen.[16]

References: (1) Psalm 37:3-4; (2) Psalm 19:13; (3) Psalm 19:14; (4) Psalm 37:5; (5) Psalm 10:17; (6) Psalm 21:2; (7) Psalm 38:9; (8) Psalm 38:15; (9) Psalm 73:23; (10) Psalm 73:24; (11) Psalm 73:25; (12) Psalm 73:26; (13) Psalm 145:18; (14) Psalm 145:19; (15) Psalm 145:19; (16) John 16:23.

15
Enlightenment

Prayer Purpose: To thank God for enlightening you and to ask Him for help to walk in the light He provides for you.

Key Scripture: *"The Lord is my light and my salvation; whom shall I fear? The Lord is the strength of my life; of whom shall I be afraid?"* (Ps. 27:1).

Prayer: Lord God, thank you for being my light and my salvation. The knowledge of this truth keeps me from all fear. Thank you, also, for being the strength of my life.[1] Your Word is a lamp unto my feet and a light unto my path, dear God. Help me to walk in the light it sheds each step of the way.[2]

I ask you, Father, to lift up the light of your countenance upon me.[3] Thank you so much for putting gladness in my heart,[4] and for enabling me to lie down in safety.[5] Light my candle and enlighten me, O Lord God. Drive out any darkness from my life, I pray.[6] Thank you for hearing and answering my prayer.

How excellent is your lovingkindness, O God. I place my full trust in you.[7] Thank you for abundantly satisfying me and meeting my needs. It is so good to drink from the river of your pleasures.[8]

With you, dear Father, is the fountain of life, and in your light I am able to see light.[9] Thank you for enlightening me, dear God.

O send out your light and your truth. Let them lead me and bring me unto your holy hill and to the tabernacle of your presence.[10] Thank you for enabling me to experience your joy and to know your joyful sound, O God. Let me ever walk in the light of your countenance.[11]

In your name I shall rejoice all day long,[12] for you are the glory of my strength.[13] Thank you, Father, for being my defense and my King.[14] With your help, I will walk in your light forever. You shall always be the light of my life.

In Jesus' righteous name I pray, Amen.[15]

References: (1) Psalm 27:1; (2) Psalm 119:105; (3) Psalm 4:6; (4) Psalm 4:7; (5) Psalm 4:8; (6) Psalm 18:28; (7) Psalm 36:7; (8) Psalm 36:8; (9) Psalm 36:9; (10) Psalm 43:3; (11) Psalm 89:15; (12) Psalm 89:16; (13) Psalm 89:17; (14) Psalm 89:18; (15) John 15:16.

16

Faithfulness

Prayer Purpose: To remind yourself of God's faithfulness to you and to ask Him to help you become more faithful.

Key Scripture: *"Oh, love the Lord, all you His saints! For the Lord preserves the faithful....Be of good courage, and He shall strengthen your heart, all you who hope in the Lord"* (Ps. 31:23-24, NKJV).

Prayer: O Lord God, my Father, I love you with all my heart, and I thank you for the certain knowledge that you will preserve me, as I am faithful to you.[1] Help me to be faithful to you at all times, dear God. With your help I will be of good courage, because I know you shall strengthen my heart as I hope in you.[2] Thank you, Father.

Truly my soul waits upon you, O God,[3] for you only are my Rock, my salvation, and my defense. For this reason I know that I shall not be moved, and this fills me with great faith.[4] Thank you, Father. Help me to be faithful to you and your Word at all times.

Father, you are always faithful, and I want to be like you. I will sing of your mercies forever, and with my mouth I will make your faithfulness known to all generations.[5] Help me do this faithfully. Let your faithfulness and mercy be with me always, dear God.[6]

It is a good thing to give thanks to you, Father, and to sing praises to your name.[7] Help me to be faithful to declare your lovingkindness every morning and your faithfulness every night.[8]

Your Word is a lamp unto my feet and a light unto my path.[9] Thank you for your faithful Word, Father, which is settled forever in heaven.[10] It proclaims your faithfulness to me.

Indeed, your faithfulness is unto all generations.[11] Thank you for your great faithfulness to me, dear God.

I enter into your gates with thanksgiving and I go into your courts with praise, for I am so very thankful to you, Father, and I want always to be faithful in blessing your name.[12]

You are so good and faithful. Your mercy is everlasting, and your truth endures to all generations.[13] Help me to be your faithful servant forever.

In the faithful name of Jesus I pray, Amen.[14]

References: *(1) Psalm 31:23; (2) Psalm 31:24; (3) Psalm 62:1; (4) Psalm 62:2; (5) Psalm 89:1; (6) Psalm 89:24; (7) Psalm 92:1; (8) Psalm 92:2; (9) Psalm 119:105; (10) Psalm 119:89; (11) Psalm 119:90; (12) Psalm 100:4; (13) Psalm 119:90; (14) John 16:23.*

17

Fear

Prayer Purpose: To ask God to deliver you from all fear and to thank Him for doing so.

Key Scripture: *"God is our refuge and strength, a very present help in trouble. Therefore we will not fear, even though the earth be removed, and though the mountains be carried into the midst of the sea"* (Ps. 46:1-2, NKJV).

Prayer: Heavenly Father, you are my refuge, my strength, and a very present help in times of trouble and fear. Knowing this, therefore, I will not fear, no matter what comes my way.[1] Help me to overcome all fear in my life, dear God.

You are my light and my salvation. Whom shall I fear? You are the strength of my life. Of whom shall I be afraid?[2]

It gives me great peace of mind, Father, to realize that in the time of trouble you will hide me in your pavilion. In the secret place of your tabernacle you will hide me; and you shall set me high upon a rock.[3] Thank you so much for this assurance from your Word.

I praise you for your Word, dear God, for I have placed my trust in you and your Word. Your Word declares that, though I walk through the valley of the shadow of death, I will fear no evil, for you are with me.[4]

Therefore, I will not fear what others might attempt to do to me.[5] I have placed all my trust in you, Father, and this keeps me from all fear.[6]

Thank you for freeing me from fear. Anytime I am tempted to fear, I will trust in you.[7]

Father, I choose to dwell in your secret place and to abide under your shadow.[8] You are my refuge and my fortress, and I will trust in you.[9] Thank you for your protection and for providing me with a place of safety under your wings, in the shelter of your presence. I will ever trust in you, Almighty God.[10]

Thank you for delivering me from fear. Help me to walk in that deliverance and to know that I need not be afraid any longer.[11] You, dear Father, are my refuge and my habitation, and you have given your angels charge over me to keep me in all my ways.[12] Thank you so much. I have set my love upon you, and I know you will always deliver me.[13]

As I call upon you, dear Father, I know you will answer me. I know, also, that you will always be with me in times of trouble and fear. Thank you for your promise to deliver me and honor me.[14] In Jesus' blessed name I pray, Amen.[15]

References: *(1) Psalm 46:1-2; (2) Psalm 27:1; (3) Psalm 27:5; (4) Psalm 23:4; (5) Psalm 56:4; (6) Psalm 56:11; (7) Psalm 56:3; (8) Psalm 91:1; (9) Psalm 91:2; (10) Psalm 91:4; (11) Psalm 91:3; (12) Psalm 91:11; (13) Psalm 91:14; (14) Psalm 91:15; (15) John 15:16.*

18
Gladness

Prayer Purpose: To remind yourself of the gladness God has imparted to you and to thank Him for making you glad.

Key Scripture: *"I will praise You, O Lord, with my whole heart; I will tell of all Your marvelous works. I will be glad and rejoice in You; I will sing praise to Your name, O Most High"* (Ps. 9:1-2, NKJV).

Prayer: Most high God, I praise you with my whole heart, as you reveal your marvelous works in and through my life. Indeed, I will be glad and rejoice in you, as I sing praise to your great name.[1]

Thank you for putting gladness in my heart.[2] I will lie down in peace and sleep restfully, because I know you are keeping me safe.[3] Thank you, Father.

You have anointed me with the oil of gladness, dear God, and my heart is filled with gratitude.[4] Knowing how you have blessed me with so many wonderful things, I will joyfully praise you, as I endeavor to serve you with gladness and come before your presence with singing.[5]

Lord God, I have set you always before me. Because I know you are at my right hand, I will not be moved.[6] Therefore, my heart is

143

glad, and I am filled with rejoicing. You have made it possible for me to rest in hope, dear Father.[7] Thank you so much.

Thank you for your abiding promise to show me the path of life. In your presence, dear God, there is fullness of joy, and at your right hand there are pleasures forevermore.[8] Help me ever to be glad in you, Father, and even to shout for joy.[9]

Because of the gladness you've given to me, I will praise your name with a song, and I will magnify you with thanksgiving.[10] It is a good thing to give thanks to you, O Lord God, and to sing praises to your name.[11]

You have done so many great things for me, and the knowledge of your goodness and faithfulness in my life truly makes me glad.[12] Thank you, Father, for giving me so much to be glad about. In the loving name of Jesus I pray, Amen.[13]

References: (1) Psalm 9:1-2; (2) Psalm 4:7; (3) Psalm 4:8; (4) Psalm 45:7; (5) Psalm 100:1-2; (6) Psalm 16:8; (7) Psalm 16:9; (8) Psalm 16:11; (9) Psalm 33:3; (10) Psalm 69:30; (11) Psalm 92:1; (12) Psalm 126:3; (13) John 15:16.

19

God's Goodness

Prayer Purpose: To reflect on God's goodness to you and to express your appreciation for His goodness in your life.

Key Scripture: *"Surely goodness and mercy shall follow me all the days of my life: and I will dwell in the house of the Lord for ever"* (Ps. 23:6).

Prayer: Father, I thank you for your goodness and for your promises that goodness and mercy shall follow me all the days of my life and I will dwell in your house forever.[1] I believe your Word, and I claim these promises for my life right now. Thank you for revealing your goodness to me.[2]

Oh, how great is your goodness, Father, which you have laid up for all those who trust and reverence you.[3] Thank you for the inheritance of your goodness in my life. Your Word is right, and all your works are done in truth, dear God. I thank you that the whole earth is filled with your goodness.[4] Praise you, Father.

Your goodness endures forever.[5] I will praise you always, because of your goodness.[6] I praise you now, Father, for your goodness to me and for your wonderful works in my life.[7] Thank you for satisfying my longing soul and filling my hungry soul with goodness.[8]

Blessed are you, O Lord God, for you are my strength, my fortress, my high tower, my Deliverer, and my shield. I place all my trust in you and your goodness.[9]

I extol you with high praises, my God, O King, and I will bless your name forever and ever. Every day I will bless you, and I will praise your name forever and ever. You are so great that your greatness truly is unsearchable.[10] Thank you, Father, for your goodness and your greatness in my life. In the good and holy name of Jesus I pray, Amen.[11]

References: (1) Psalm 23:6; (2) Psalm 27:13; (3) Psalm 31:19; (4) Psalm 33:4-5; (5) Psalm 52:1; (6) Psalm 52:9; (7) Psalm 107:8; (8) Psalm 107:9; (9) Psalm 144:1-2; (10) Psalm 145:1-3; (11) John 15:16.

20

God's Greatness

Prayer Purpose: To reflect on God's greatness and to thank Him for being such a great God to you.

Key Scripture: *"Great is the Lord, and greatly to be praised in the city of our God, in the mountain of his holiness. Beautiful for situation, the joy of the whole earth, is mount Zion, on the sides of the north, the city of the great King"* (Ps. 48:1-2).

Prayer: Great are You, O God, my King and my Lord. I take strength from knowing how great you are, and I praise you with all my heart.[1] You are my strength and my shield.

My heart safely trusts in you, Father, and I realize you are helping me. My heart greatly rejoices in you, and I praise you with singing and joy.[2]

Thank you for being my strength, dear God.[3] I extol you, my God and my King, and I will bless your name forever.[4]

Every day I will bless you, and I will praise your name forever.[5] You are so great, Lord God, and you are greatly to be praised. Truly, your greatness is unsearchable.[6]

O Lord my God, you are very great. You are clothed with splendor and majesty. You cover yourself with light as with a garment and stretch out the heavens like a curtain. You make the clouds your chariot and ride on the wings of the wind. You set the earth on its foundation; it can never be moved.[7]

I will speak of the glorious honor of your majesty and of all your wondrous works, dear Father.[8] Wherever I go, I will declare your greatness.[9] Thank you for being so gracious to me. You are full of compassion, slow to anger, and of great mercy.[10] Thank you, Lord God.

How I praise you, mighty God, for your greatness, for you are good to all, and your tender mercies are over all your works.[11] In fact, all of your works shall praise you, Father.[12] Help me to remember always to speak of the glory of your kingdom and to talk of your mighty power.[13]

Father, thank you for the truth that your kingdom is an everlasting kingdom, and your dominion endures throughout all generations.[14] I rejoice in your greatness, dear God.

In the all-powerful name of your Son, Jesus Christ, I pray, Amen.[15]

References: (1) *Psalm 48:1-2; (2) Psalm 28:7; (3) Psalm 28:8; (4) Psalm 145:1; (5) Psalm 145:2; (6) Psalm 145:3; (7) Psalm 104:1-5; (8) Psalm 145:5; (9) Psalm 145:6; (10) Psalm 145:8; (11) Psalm 145:9; (12) Psalm 145:10; (13) Psalm 145:11; (14) Psalm 145:13; (15) John 16:23.*

21
God's Lovingkindness

Prayer Purpose: To reflect on God's lovingkindness in your life and to thank Him for loving you so much.

Key Scripture: *"How excellent is thy lovingkindness, O God! Therefore the children of men put their trust under the shadow of thy wings"* (Ps. 36:7).

Prayer: Father God, your lovingkindness in my life is so excellent. Because I know you love me, I am able to trust you.[1] Thank you for your love.

I know you will hear me, O Lord God, for your lovingkindness is so wonderful. Turn to me now according to the multitude of your tender mercies.[2] I place all my trust in you, Father.

I ask that you would let your truth and your lovingkindness continually preserve me.[3] Because your lovingkindness is better than life to me, my lips shall always praise you, Father.[4] I will ever bless you as long as I live, and I will lift up my hands in your name.[5]

Help me to show forth your lovingkindness in the morning and your faithfulness every night.[6] Thank you for forgiving all my iniquities, Father, and for healing all my diseases.[7] Thank you, also, for redeeming my life from destruction and crowning me with your lovingkindness and tender mercies.[8]

Quicken me with your life, Father, according to your lovingkindness, that I would be able to keep all your testimonies.[9] Cause me to hear your lovingkindness in the morning, for in you do I trust. Cause me to know the way in which I should walk, for I lift up my soul to you.[10] Teach me to do your will, dear God, for you are my loving Father.[11]

In the loving name of Jesus I pray, Amen.[12]

References: *(1) Psalm 36:7; (2) Psalm 69:16; (3) Psalm 40:11; (4) Psalm 63:3; (5) Psalm 63:4; (6) Psalm 92:2; (7) Psalm 103:3; (8) Psalm 103:4; (9) Psalm 119:88; (10) Psalm 143:8; (11) Psalm 143:10; (12) John 15:16.*

22

God's Mercy

Prayer Purpose: To reflect on God's tender mercies in your life and to thank Him for being your merciful Father.

Key Scripture: *"I will sing of the mercies of the Lord for ever: with my mouth will I make known thy faithfulness to all generations"* (Ps. 89:1).

Prayer: Dear God, thank you for your great mercy in my life. I will sing of your mercies forever, and I will make your faithfulness known to all generations.[1] Father, I trust in your mercy completely, and I rejoice in the salvation you've given to me.[2] I will sing unto you, because you have dealt so bountifully with me.[3]

Through your mercy, dear God, I know I shall never be moved.[4] Thank you so much for your mercy. All of your paths are mercy and truth to me,[5] and I know your mercy and goodness shall follow me all the days of my life.[6] Thank you, Father.

I am glad, and I rejoice in your mercy.[7] Thank you for promising me that your mercy shall surround me at all times.[8] Therefore, I will remain glad in you, Father, and I will always greatly rejoice in your mercy.[9] Let your wonderful mercy be upon me, as I continue to hope in you.[10]

Help me, Father, to trust in your mercy forever.[11] Thank you for being so merciful and gracious to me. I am so grateful that you are slow to anger and abound in mercy.[12]

As the heavens are high above the earth, so great are your love and mercy to me. Thank you so much that you have removed my transgressions from me, even as far as the east is from the west.[13] Deal with me according to your mercy, and teach me your statutes.[14]

I give thanks to you, Lord God, for I know that your mercy endures forever.[15] You are my God, and I will praise you and exalt you.[16] You are so good to me, Father, and I rejoice to know that your mercy will last forever.[17]

In Jesus' merciful name I pray, Amen.[18]

References: (1) Psalm 89:1; (2) Psalm 13:5; (3) Psalm 13:6; (4) Psalm 21:7; (5) Psalm 25:10; (6) Psalm 23:6; (7) Psalm 31:7; (8) Psalm 32:10; (9) Psalm 32:11; (10) Psalm 33:22; (11) Psalm 52:8; (12) Psalm 103:8; (13) Psalm 103:11-12; (14) Psalm 119:124; (15) Psalm 118:1; (16) Psalm 118:28; (17) Psalm 118:29; (18) John 16:23.

23

God's Power and Might

Prayer Purpose: To reflect on God's omnipotence and to thank Him for His power, which is at work in your life.

Key Scripture: *"But I will sing of Your power; yes, I will sing aloud of Your mercy in the morning; for You have been my defense and refuge in the day of my trouble. To You, O my Strength, I will sing praises; for God is my defense, and my God of mercy"* (Ps. 59:16-17, NKJV).

Prayer: O Lord my God, I will sing of your power and your mercy, for you have been and are my defense and my refuge.[1] Thank you for revealing your power and might to me.

Power belongs to you, Father, and I greatly rejoice in your power and strength.[2] Through the greatness of your power, your enemies shall submit themselves unto you, and all the earth shall worship you.[3]

I worship you as my Lord and King, O God, because I know you rule by your mighty power forever.[4] Give me your strength and power, dear God, I pray.[5]

There is no one like you, O God, for you have done so many great things.[6] Help me to go forth in your might and strength,[7] and declare your strength to this generation and your power to succeeding generations, as well.[8]

Your power is incomprehensibly great, O God, and your understanding is infinite.[9] Therefore, I will extol you with high praise, my God, O King, and I will bless your name forever and ever.[10]

Every day I will bless you, and I will praise your name forever.[11] Thank you for being my great God and King and Father. Truly, your greatness is unsearchable.[12]

In the mighty name of Jesus I pray, Amen.[13]

References: (1) Psalm 59:16-17; (2) Psalm 62:11; (3) Psalm 66:3-4; (4) Psalm 66:7; (5) Psalm 68:35; (6) Psalm 71:19; (7) Psalm 71:16; (8) Psalm 71:18; (9) Psalm 147:5; (10) Psalm 145:1; (11) Psalm 145:2; (12) Psalm 145:3; (13) John 15:16.

24

God's Wisdom

Prayer Purpose: To reflect on God's great wisdom and to ask Him to give you the wisdom you need.

Key Scripture: *"Hear this, all ye people; give ear, all ye inhabitants of the world: both low and high, rich and poor, together. My mouth shall speak of wisdom: and the meditation of my heart shall be of understanding"* (Ps. 49:1-3).

Prayer: O God, my heavenly Father, help me always to speak of wisdom and to seek the understanding you desire to impart to me from your Word.[1] I need your wisdom, and I ask you to help me know your wisdom deep within.[2] Therefore, I ask you to teach me to number and manage my days, Father, so I will be able to apply my heart to the wisdom you give to me.[3]

Remembering that reverential fear and honor of you, Father, was the beginning of wisdom in my life, help me to obey your Word and your commands at all times.[4] This, I know, will give me greater understanding of you and your ways.[5] Thank you, Father, for hearing and answering my prayer.

Help me always to delight in your Word, O Lord God, and to meditate therein both night and day.[6] I want to be like a tree planted by the rivers of water, and I want to bring forth fruit. Help me, Father, to be fruitful and prosperous in whatever I do.[7]

Light my candle and enlighten my heart, Father, and bring your light into the world of darkness that surrounds me.[8] Your way is perfect, I realize, and your Word is tried and true. Thank you for being a mighty Buckler for me.[9]

Teach me, O God, the way of your statutes, so I will always keep them.[10] Give me your wisdom and understanding, as I endeavor to keep your Word and observe your teachings with my whole heart.[11]

Lead me in the path of your commandments, for I find my delight in them.[12] Thank you for your promise that those who love your law have great peace.[13]

Give me understanding and wisdom, and I shall live.[14] Hear my cry, Lord God, and give me understanding and wisdom according to your Word,[15] for I recognize that your Word is a lamp unto my feet and a light unto my path.[16]

In the name of my Savior, Jesus, I pray, Amen.[17]

References: (1) Psalm 49:1-3; (2) Psalm 51:6; (3) Psalm 90:12; (4) Psalm 111:10; (5) Psalm 111:10; (6) Psalm 1:2; (7) Psalm 1:3; (8) Psalm 18:28; (9) Psalm 18:30; (10) Psalm 119:33; (11) Psalm 119:34; (12) Psalm 119:35; (13) Psalm 119:165; (14) Psalm 119:144; (15) Psalm 119:169; (16) Psalm 119:105; (17) John 16:23.

25

God's Word

Prayer Purpose: To reflect on the importance of God's Word and to thank Him for the power of His Word in your life.

Key Scripture: *"How can a young man cleanse his way? By taking heed according to Your word....Your word I have hidden in my heart, that I might not sin against You"* (Ps. 119:9-11, NKJV).

Prayer: Dear Father, help me ever to remember to hide your Word in my heart and to keep my life pure by living according to your Word, that I might not sin against you.[1] Deal bountifully with me, that I may live and keep your Word.[2]

Oh, how I love your Word! It is my meditation throughout the day.[3] Thank you for giving me wisdom through your Word.[4]

Open my eyes, that I may always behold wondrous things out of your Word.[5]

Your Word, O Father, is a lamp unto my feet and a light unto my path.[6] Help me to walk in its truth and light at all times. Teach me the way of your statutes, and help me to keep them throughout my life.[7]

Give me understanding, and I shall keep your law. Help me to observe the truth of your Word with my whole heart.[8]

Direct me in the path of all your com-mandments, Father, for I take great delight in each one of them.[9] Incline my heart to your Word,[10] and establish your Word within me.[11]

Your Word, O Father, is settled forever in heaven.[12] Therefore, I will not forget your precepts. Thank you for the life you've imparted to me through your Word.[13]

How sweet your words are to my taste, dear God.[14] The entrance of your words give light and understanding to me.[15] Thank you so much for your Word, dear God.

In Jesus' all-powerful name I pray, Amen.[16]

References: *(1) Psalm 119:9-11; (2) Psalm 119:17; (3) Psalm 119:97; (4) Psalm 119:98; (5) Psalm 119:18; (6) Psalm 119:105; (7) Psalm 119:33; (8) Psalm 119:34; (9) Psalm 119:35; (10) Psalm 119:36; (11) Psalm 119:38; (12) Psalm 119:89; (13) Psalm 119:93; (14) Psalm 119:103; (15) Psalm 119:130; (16) John 15:16.*

26

Grief and Mourning

Prayer Purpose: To ask God to sustain you and comfort you in your time of loss.

Key Scripture: *"Yea, though I walk through the valley of the shadow of death, I will fear no evil: for thou art with me; thy rod and thy staff they comfort me"* (Ps. 23:4).

Prayer: O God, my heavenly Father, I ask you to give me your comfort, as I experience grief and mourning over the loss of _____. Thank you for your promise to be with me.[1]

Have mercy upon me, Father, for I am weak.[2] My soul is vexed and troubled.[3] I am weary as a result of my grief.[4]

Preserve me, O God, for I put my trust in you.[5] You, Father God, are my refuge and my strength, and you are a very present help to me during this time of loss and mourning.[6] Thank you for always being there for me; I know you are with me.[7]

I believe you are the God who does wonders.[8] Bow down your ear, dear Father, and hear me, for I really need your help.[9] Preserve my soul.[10]

Be merciful unto me.[11] Give ear, O Lord God, to my prayer, and attend to the voice of my supplications.[12]

I call upon you, because I know you will answer me.[13] Thank you for being full of compassion, gracious, longsuffering, and abundant in mercy and in truth.[14] Turn unto me, and give me your strength.[15] Thank you, Father.

Help me to lie down in green pastures, and lead me beside the still waters.[16] Father, restore my soul, and lead me in the paths of righteousness for your name's sake.[17]

Thank you for your goodness and mercy, which will follow me all the days of my life.[18] I choose to believe your Word, dear God, and I believe you are enabling me to overcome all grief and mourning.

In Jesus' name I pray, Amen.[19]

References: *(1) Psalm 23:4; (2) Psalm 6:2; (3) Psalm 6:3; (4) Psalm 6:6; (5) Psalm 16:1; (6) Psalm 46:1; (7) Psalm 46:7; (8) Psalm 77:14; (9) Psalm 86:1; (10) Psalm 86:2; (11) Psalm 86:3; (12) Psalm 86:6; (13) Psalm 86:7; (14) Psalm 86:15; (15) Psalm 86:16; (16) Psalm 23:2; (17) Psalm 23:3; (18) Psalm 23:6; (19) John 16:23.*

27

Guidance

Prayer Purpose: To ask God to lead and guide you and to thank Him for doing so.

Key Scripture: *"I will instruct you and teach you in the way you should go; I will guide you with My eye"* (Ps. 32:8, NKJV).

Prayer: Heavenly Father, thank you for your promise to instruct me, teach me, and guide me.[1] I claim this promise for my life right now, and I ask you to lead me beside the still waters and in the paths of righteousness for your name's sake.[2]

You are so good and upright, dear God, and I ask you to teach me your ways.[3] In meekness, I beseech you to guide me each step of my way.[4]

I thank you for being my Rock and my fortress. Therefore, for your name's sake, I ask you to lead me and guide me at all times.[5]

Thank you for being my God and my Guide forever.[6] I need your guidance in my life, dear Father, right now and always.

Guide me with your counsel, dear God.[7] How I praise you that your Word is a lamp unto my feet and a light unto my path.[8] Help me to walk in the light of your Word, as I continue my journey with you. Feed me according to your integrity, and guide me by the skillfulness of your hands.[9]

Lead me, O Lord God, in your righteousness. Make your way straight before my face.[10] Show me your ways, and teach me your paths.[11] Lead me in your truth, and teach me, for you are the God of my salvation, and I wait on you all day.[12]

Search me, O God, and know my heart. Try me, and know my thoughts, and see if there be any wicked way in me. Lead me in your everlasting way.[13] In Jesus' precious name I pray, Amen.[14]

References: (1) Psalm 32:8; (2) Psalm 23:2-3; (3) Psalm 25:8; (4) Psalm 25:9; (5) Psalm 31:3; (6) Psalm 48:14; (7) Psalm 73:24; (8) Psalm 119:105; (9) Psalm 78:72; (10) Psalm 5:8; (11) Psalm 25:4; (12) Psalm 25:5; (13) Psalm 139:23-24; (14) John 15:16.

28

Happiness

Prayer Purpose: To express your happiness to God and to thank Him for making you happy.

Key Scripture: *"Happy is he who has the God of Jacob for his help, whose hope is in the Lord his God, who made heaven and earth, the sea, and all that is in them; who keeps truth forever"* (Ps. 146:5-6, NKJV).

Prayer: O God, you are my Lord, and in you I find great hope and happiness.[1] Thank you for the happiness I enjoy as your child. Help me to walk in your ways, in reverential fear and awe of you.

Thank you, Father, for making it possible for me to find fulfillment in the work I do and to receive your promises of happiness and well-being.[2] I believe and receive your promises now, as I pray.

Because I have found you as my God and King, I now experience full and complete happiness in you.[3] Thank you, Father.

I trust you with all my heart, Lord God. Your faithfulness makes me want to shout for joy and happiness. I love your name and find joy in you.[4] Thank you for the joy and happiness you've imparted to me.

My soul is happy and joyful in you, Father God, and I greatly rejoice because of the salvation you've provided for me through your Son, Jesus Christ.[5]

Because your lovingkindness is better than life to me, my lips shall praise you.[6] I will bless you, Father God, while I live, and I will lift up my hands in your name.[7]

I believe and receive your promise that my soul shall be satisfied. Therefore, I praise you with joyful lips.[8] Thank you for always being my source of help, Father.

I will ever rejoice in your presence, under the shadow of your wings, dear Lord God.[9] Thank you again for the great happiness and joy I now experience.

Lord God, I set you always before me. I thank you that you are at my right hand, and this certainty causes me to know that I shall never be moved.[10] Thank you, Father. Because this is true, my heart is glad and I am able to rest in hope.[11]

It is so wonderful to realize that you have shown me the path of life, dear God. In your glorious presence there is always fullness of joy, and at your right hand I experience pleasures forevermore.[12] Thank you for making me so happy, dear Father.

In the blessed name of your Son, Jesus Christ, I pray, Amen.[13]

References: (1) Psalm 146:5-6; (2) Psalm 128:1-2; (3) Psalm 144:15; (4) Psalm 5:11; (5) Psalm 35:9; (6) Psalm 63:3; (7) Psalm 63:4; (8) Psalm 63:5; (9) Psalm 63:7; (10) Psalm 16:8; (11) Psalm 16:9; (12) Psalm 16:11; (13) John 15:16.

29

Healing

Prayer Purpose: To ask God to heal you of any illnesses or afflictions in your body and to thank Him for His healing power.

Key Scripture: *"Bless the Lord, O my soul; and all that is within me, bless His holy name! Bless the Lord, O my soul, and forget not all His benefits: who forgives all your iniquities, who heals all your diseases, who redeems your life from destruction, who crowns you with lovingkindness and tender mercies, who satisfies your mouth with good things, so that your youth is renewed like the eagle's"* (Ps. 103:1-5, NKJV).

Prayer: Have mercy on me, O Lord God. I need your healing touch, and I ask you to heal me as I pray.[1] Thank you for the promises of healing I find in your Word, dear God.

I bless you, Lord God. With all that is within me, I bless your holy name, and I do not forget all your benefits to me. You forgive all my iniquities and heal all my diseases. You redeem my life from destruction and crown me with lovingkindness and tender mercies. You satisfy my mouth with good things, so that my youth is renewed like the eagle's.[2]

I will praise you, for I believe you are lifting me up and healing me, as I pray to you.[3] Thank you, Father God.

As I cry unto you, I ask you to send your Word and heal me,[4] for I believe the assurance your Word gives to me, that you will protect me from all diseases and pestilences.[5]

Thank you, Father, for permitting me to dwell in your secret place and to abide under the shadow of your presence.[6]

I rejoice in the protection from illnesses and diseases that you are giving to me. I believe your Word, which assures me that you will cover me with your feathers and your protection, and your truth shall be my shield and buckler.[7]

I believe your promise, dear God, that, as I make you my refuge and my habitation, you will bring me into your place of care and protection, where no evil shall befall me and no disease shall come near me.[8]

Thank you, Father, for this promise and for the angelic protection I now enjoy.[9] I set my love upon you, and I know the might and power of your name.[10]

As I call upon you now, I know you will answer me and be with me. I believe and receive your promise to deliver me and to give me long life.[11] Thank you, Father.

I place my hope for healing in you, O God, and I praise you for healing me. Thank you for being the health of my countenance and my God forever.[12]

In the powerful name of Jesus I pray, Amen.[13]

References: *(1) Psalm 6:2; (2) Psalm 103:1-5; (3) Psalm 30:1-2; (4) Psalm 107:20; (5) Psalm 91:3; (6) Psalm 91:1; (7) Psalm 91:4; (8) Psalm 91:10; (9) Psalm 91:11-12; (10) Psalm 91:14; (11) Psalm 91:15-16; (12) Psalm 42:11; (13) John 16:23.*

30

Help

Prayer Purpose: To seek divine aid in your time of need and to thank God for helping you in so many ways.

Key Scripture: *"Our soul waits for the Lord; He is our help and our shield. For our heart shall rejoice in Him, because we have trusted in His holy name. Let Your mercy, O Lord, be upon us, just as we hope in You"* (Ps. 33:20-23, NKJV).

Prayer: O Lord God, my soul waits for you, because I know you are my help and my shield. Realizing this, my heart rejoices in you, and I trust in your most holy name. Let your mercy be upon me, as I place all my hope in you.[1]

Thank you for being my strength in time of trouble.[2] I know you will always help me, Father, and I believe you will always deliver me.[3] Thank you for all the promises of your Word.

Lord God, there is so much comfort and peace in knowing that you are my refuge and strength — a very present help to me in times of difficulty. Because I know these things are true, I will not fear.[4] Thank you for being with me.[5]

I need your help in my life, Father, in the following areas:

_____

_____

_____.

I receive your help by faith, knowing that, through you I shall do valiantly, for you are the One who treads down all my enemies.[6]

As I lift up my eyes to you, I recognize more fully than ever before that all my help comes from you, O God.[7] I believe and receive your promise that you will never slumber nor ever permit my foot to be moved.[8]

Thank you, Father, for being my Keeper.[9] Preserve me from all evil, I pray.[10] Preserve my going out and my coming in from this time forth and forevermore.[11]

Thank you for being my help and my shield, Lord God.[12]

In the precious name of Jesus, your Son, I pray, Amen.[13]

References: *(1) Psalm 33:20-22; (2) Psalm 37:39; (3) Psalm 37:40; (4) Psalm 46:1-2; (5) Psalm 46:5; (6) Psalm 60:11-12; (7) Psalm 121:1-2; (8) Psalm 121:3; (9) Psalm 121:7; (10) Psalm 121:7; (11) Psalm 121:8; (12) Psalm 115:9; (13) John 15:16.*

31
Hope

Prayer Purpose: To express your hope in God and to ask Him to make you even more hopeful.

Key Scripture: *"For You are my hope, O Lord God; You are my trust from my youth"* (Ps. 71:5, NKJV).

Prayer: O Lord God, you are my hope, and I fully trust in you.[1] In you I place all my hope, Father, for I know you are hearing and answering my prayers.[2]

Thank you for imparting hope to me. With your help, I will hope continually, and I will be sure to praise you more and more.[3]

Thank you for your Word and all its promises in which I place my hope firmly and securely.[4] When pressures invade my life, your glorious Word fills me with hope, Father.[5]

You are my hiding place and my shield, and I choose to hope in your Word.[6] Uphold me according to your Word, so I will never be ashamed.[7]

I cry unto you, Lord God.[8] Hear my voice, and let your ears be attentive unto my supplications.[9] I wait for you, Father, as I continue to hope in your Word and your marvelous promises to me.[10]

Thank you for restoring my hope and giving me great happiness, dear God.[11] I place all of my hope in you, for I know you are the Creator of all things and you love me.[12] I rejoice in the hope your Word gives to me, dear Father.[13]

In the magnificent name of Jesus I pray, Amen.[14]

References: *(1) Psalm 71:5; (2) Psalm 38:15; (3) Psalm 71:14; (4) Psalm 119:49; (5) Psalm 119:81; (6) Psalm 119:114; (7) Psalm 119:116; (8) Psalm 130:1; (9) Psalm 130:2; (10) Psalm 130:5; (11) Psalm 146:5; (12) Psalm 146:6; (13) Psalm 119:162; (14) John 15:16.*

32

Inheritance

Prayer Purpose: To thank God for the inheritance He has prepared for you and to reflect on all His blessings in your life.

Key Scripture: *"O Lord, You are the portion of my inheritance and my cup; You maintain my lot"* (Ps. 16:5, NKJV).

Prayer: O Lord God, preserve me, for in you I have placed my trust.[1] You are my chosen inheritance. Thank you for maintaining that which I've so freely inherited from your hands.[2]

I believe your promise that the rich inheritance you've bestowed upon me shall last forever.[3] Thank you, Father.

My soul truly dwells at ease as I contemplate your promise that I shall inherit the earth, along with all your people.[4] Thank you for sharing your secrets with me and revealing your covenant to me.[5] Father, your covenant is so precious to me.

Help me, Father God, to trust in you and do your will in my life. As I do so, I know I shall dwell in the land you've given to me, and I know you will feed me.[6]

I delight myself in you, Father, and I thank you for promising to give me the desires of my heart.[7] I believe and receive your promise now.

I willingly choose to commit my way to you, Lord God, and to trust completely in you. As I do so, I know I will receive the inheritance you've prepared for me.[8] Thank you, Father. I trust you to bring forth my righteousness as the light.[9]

Therefore, I rest in you securely and wait patiently for you.[10]

Enable me to walk in meekness, Lord God, for I realize that the meek shall inherit the earth and shall delight themselves in the abundance of peace you give to them.[11] Thank you, Father, for your peace.

My delight is in your Word, which is an inherited treasure I've received from your hands. Help me to meditate in your Word both night and day.[12] I rejoice to know that you will help me to become like a tree planted by the rivers of water.

Thank you for your promise that you will enable me to bring forth my fruit in its proper season. Thank you, also, for the promise of prosperity, Father.[13]

I am thrilled by the inheritance I've received from your hands. Thank you so much for giving me so much.

In Jesus' name I pray, Amen.[14]

References: (1) Psalm 16:1; (2) Psalm 16:5; (3) Psalm 37:18; (4) Psalm 25:13; (5) Psalm 25:14; (6) Psalm 37:3; (7) Psalm 37:4; (8) Psalm 37:5; (9) Psalm 37:6; (10) Psalm 37:7; (11) Psalm 37:11; (12) Psalm 1:2; (13) Psalm 1:3; (14) John 16:23.

33

Integrity

Prayer Purpose: To ask God to help you walk in integrity throughout your life and to thank Him for making this possible.

Key Scripture: *"Keep my soul, and deliver me; let me not be ashamed, for I put my trust in You. Let integrity and uprightness preserve me, for I wait for You"* (Ps. 25:20-21, NKJV).

Prayer: Heavenly Father, I ask you to keep my soul and deliver me. Don't ever let me be ashamed, for I put my trust in you. Let integrity and uprightness preserve me, for I wait on you.[1]

Judge me, O Lord God, according to the righteousness and integrity you've imparted to me in Christ Jesus.[2] Thank you for enabling me to walk in integrity, Father.

Your lovingkindness is ever before me, and I desire to walk in your truth.[3] Therefore, I choose to go forth in the integrity you've enabled me to have. As I do so, Father, be merciful to me.[4]

Uphold me in my integrity, and set me before your face forever.[5] Feed me according to the integrity of your heart, and guide me by the skillfulness of your hands.[6]

Oh, that my ways were directed to keep your statutes at all times, dear Father.[7] This truly is the cry of my heart, because I realize that by walking in the light your Word provides to me,[8] I will never be ashamed.[9] Thank you, Father. I ask you to help me always to remember to praise you with integrity of heart.[10]

Deal bountifully with me, Father, that I may live and keep your Word at all times.[11] Open my eyes, that I may behold wondrous things in your Word.[12] Give me the grace I need to walk in integrity, through the power of your Word and your Spirit, minute by minute and day by day.

In the incomparable name of Jesus I pray, Amen.[13]

References: (1) Psalm 25:20-21; (2) Psalm 7:8; (3) Psalm 26:3; (4) Psalm 26:11; (5) Psalm 41:12; (6) Psalm 78:72; (7) Psalm 119:5; (8) Psalm 119:105; (9) Psalm 119:6; (10) Psalm 119:7; (11) Psalm 119:17; (12) Psalm 119:18; (13) John 15:16.

34

Joy

Prayer Purpose: To express your appreciation for the joy God has imparted to you.

Key Scripture: *"You will show me the path of life; in Your presence is fullness of joy; at Your right hand are pleasures forevermore"* (Ps. 16:11, NKJV).

Prayer: O God, my heavenly Father, thank you for showing me the path of life. Help me always to remember that I experience fullness of joy in your presence, and, at your right hand, there are pleasures forevermore.[1]

Thank you so much for the joy you've imparted to me. As I put all my trust in you, Father, I greatly rejoice and shout for joy, because I know you are defending me. I am joyful in you, and I love your powerful and majestic name.[2]

Thank you for your favor in my life, which surrounds me and protects me like a shield. I rejoice in the many blessings you've bestowed upon me, Lord God.[3] Your wonderful mercy encompasses me and makes me very glad in you. Indeed, it makes me want to shout for joy.[4] Thank you, Father.

O God, send out your light and your truth. Let them lead me and bring me to your holy hill and the tabernacles of your presence.[5] Father, as

I enter into your presence, you are my exceeding joy. I will ever praise you for the joy you've given to me.[6]

Let me always be satisfied with your joy and gladness, Father.[7] Help me always to walk in the joy of my salvation, and uphold me with your Spirit.[8]

Make it possible for my soul to be joyful in you at all times, Lord God, and to rejoice in the knowledge of the salvation you've given to me.[9]

O God, you are my God. Early will I seek you. My soul thirsts for you.[10] I desire to see your power and glory.[11]

Because your lovingkindness is better than life to me, I will praise you.[12] Indeed, I will bless you as long as I live, and I will lift up my hands in your name.[13]

Thank you for satisfying my soul. My mouth shall praise you with joyful lips.[14] Thank you for always being my help, dear God. I will always rejoice in the shadow of your wings.[15]

In Jesus' victorious name I pray, Amen.[16]

References: (1) Psalm 16:11; (2) Psalm 5:11; (3) Psalm 5:12; (4) Psalm 32:10-11; (5) Psalm 43:3; (6) Psalm 43:4; (7) Psalm 51:8; (8) Psalm 51:12; (9) Psalm 35:9; (10) Psalm 63:1; (11) Psalm 63:2; (12) Psalm 63:3; (13) Psalm 63:4; (14) Psalm 63:5; (15) Psalm 63:7; (16) John 16:23.

35

Loneliness

Prayer Purpose: To remind yourself that God is always with you and to ask Him to help you overcome all loneliness in your life.

Key Scripture: *"Yea, though I walk through the valley of the shadow of death, I will fear no evil: for thou art with me; thy rod and thy staff they comfort me"* (Ps. 23:4).

Prayer: Heavenly Father, help me to believe and receive all the promises of your Word during this time of loneliness in my life. Thank you for assuring me that I have no reason for fear or loneliness, because you are with me, and your presence gives me great comfort.[1] Thank you, Father.

As I dwell in the secret place you have provided for me, Lord God, under the shadow of your wings, I will reaffirm that you are my refuge and my fortress. Indeed, you are my God in whom I continually trust.[2]

Deliver me from all feelings of loneliness, dear Father.[3] Cover me with your feathers of protection, as I find my place of trust and refuge under the wings of your presence.[4]

Thank you for being my refuge and my strength, dear God. You are a very present help to me.[5] Therefore, I will not fear nor feel lonely any longer.[6]

Thank you for being in my midst and near to me. Because I know you are near, I know I shall not be moved. Thank you for your willingness to help me, Father.[7]

Help me to be still and to know that you are my God and that you are with me.[8] I receive your help as I pray, and the sense of loneliness I have been experiencing is lifting from me. Thank you, Father.

I love you, Lord God, because I know you have heard my voice and my supplications.[9] Thank you for inclining your ear unto me. Because I know you will always do so, I shall call upon you as long as I live.[10]

I rejoice in the assurance that you are delivering my soul from loneliness.[11] Thank you, Almighty God. You have delivered my soul from death, my eyes from tears, and my feet from falling.[12] In the joy of your wonderful deliverance and care, I will walk before you from now on.[13]

In Jesus' name I pray, Amen.[14]

References: *(1) Psalm 23:4; (2) Psalm 91:1-2; (3) Psalm 91:3; (4) Psalm 91:4; (5) Psalm 46:1; (6) Psalm 46:2; (7) Psalm 46:5; (8) Psalm 46:10-11; (9) Psalm 116:1; (10) Psalm 116:2; (11) Psalm 116:4; (12) Psalm 116:8; (13) Psalm 116:9; (14) John 15:16.*

36

Loving God

Prayer Purpose: To express your love to God and to thank Him for loving you.

Key Scripture: *"I will love thee, O Lord, my strength. The Lord is my rock, and my fortress, and my deliverer; my God, my strength, in whom I will trust; my buckler, and the horn of my salvation, and my high tower"* (Ps. 18:1-2).

Prayer: Lord God, my heavenly Father, I will ever love you, for you are my strength, my Rock, my fortress, my Deliverer, my God, my buckler, the horn of my salvation, and my high tower.[1] Thank you for being all these things to me. As I call upon you, I know I shall be saved from all enemies.[2]

I rejoice as I place all my trust in you, Father. I will ever shout for joy, because I know you will always defend me. I love your name, dear God. Thank you for surrounding me with your favor.[3]

Father, I love your Word. It is my meditation all day long.[4] I receive wisdom and understanding from your Word.[5] I truly love your Word above everything else, including fine gold.[6] Thank you for your Word, dear Father.

I love you so much, dear God, and I thank you for the certainty of answered prayer.[7]

Thank you, also, for inclining your ear unto me. I shall call upon you as long as I live.[8]

You are always faithful to me, Father, and I love you so much. Thank you for preserving me and rewarding me so abundantly.[9]

Dear God, I set my love upon you, knowing that, as I do so, you will deliver me and set me on high, because I know your name.[10] Thank you, Father, for this assurance.

As I call upon you, I know you will answer me. Thank you for promising to be with me always, even in times of trouble.[11]

I love you, Father, and I rejoice in the knowledge that you love me.[12] In the loving name of Jesus I pray, Amen.[13]

References: *(1) Psalm 18:1-2; (2) Psalm 18:3; (3) Psalm 5:11-12; (4) Psalm 119:97; (5) Psalm 119:98-99; (6) Psalm 119:127; (7) Psalm 116:1; (8) Psalm 116:2; (9) Psalm 31:23; (10) Psalm 91:14; (11) Psalm 91:15; (12) Psalm 63:3; (13) John 16:23.*

37

Meekness

Prayer Purpose: To ask God to help you become truly meek and to thank Him for the benefits of meekness in your life.

Key Scripture: *"But the meek shall inherit the earth; and shall delight themselves in the abundance of peace"* (Ps. 37:11).

Prayer: O God, my Father, help me to walk in meekness each and every day of my life. Thank you for all the promises of your Word, which declare so many wonderful things to those who are meek, who patiently endure and humbly acknowledge you.

I thank you, Father, for revealing to me that I shall be a part of the company of believers who shall inherit the earth. Dear God, I truly delight myself in the abundance of peace you give to me as I walk in meekness.[1]

Father, your Word assures me that the meek shall eat and be satisfied. I claim this promise now, as I praise you and seek your help. Indeed, in humility and meekness, I worship you.[2]

Thank you for supplying all of my needs. Guide me with your judgment, and teach me your way, as I endeavor to walk in meekness before you, dear God.[3]

Father, you are so great, your power is unlimited, and your understanding is infinite.[4] I praise you for your promise to lift me up when I walk in meekness before you.[5]

For all these reasons, I will sing praises unto you, Lord God, with thanksgiving.[6] I stand in reverential awe of you, Father, and I greatly hope in your mercy. It gives me great joy to know that you take pleasure in me.[7]

Thank you for strengthening the bars of my gates, and protecting and blessing my family and me.[8] I experience your peace as I pray, and I greatly enjoy all you have given to me.[9] Send forth your Word upon earth, I pray.[10]

In your majesty, dear Father, teach me how to practice meekness.[11] Now, as I pray, I claim your promises to the meek. I thank you for your promises to the meek and for hearing and answering my prayer.

In the strong name of Jesus I pray, Amen.[12]

References: (1) Psalm 37:11; (2) Psalm 22:26; (3) Psalm 25:9; (4) Psalm 147:15; (5) Psalm 147:6; (6) Psalm 147:7; (7) Psalm 147:11; (8) Psalm 147:13; (9) Psalm 147:14; (10) Psalm 147:15; (11) Psalm 45:4; (12) John 15:16.

38

Obedience

Prayer Purpose: To ask your heavenly Father to help you become a more obedient child.

Key Scripture: *"For the Lord God is a sun and shield: the Lord will give grace and glory; no good thing will he withhold from them that walk uprightly"* (Ps. 84:11).

Prayer: Dear Father, my God and my King, I ask you to help me walk in obedience every day of my life. I believe your Word, which tells me that you will give me your grace and glory, and you will not withhold any good thing from me as I walk uprightly before you.

Thank you, Lord God, for you truly are a sun and a shield to me.[1] O Lord God of hosts, hear my prayer, and give ear to me.[2]

O God, my shield, look upon my face, I pray.[3] Thank you for helping me to understand the truth that a day in your courts is better than a thousand elsewhere. Truly, Father, I would rather be a doorkeeper in your house than a dweller in the tents of wickedness.[4] That's one of the reasons why I want to become a more obedient servant to you.

Thank you so much, Lord God, for delivering my soul from death. I now ask you to help me keep my feet from falling, that I may walk before you in the land of the living.[5] O Lord God, I am your servant. Thank you for loosing my bonds.[6]

I offer to you the sacrifice of thanksgiving, as I call upon your name.[7] Cause me to hear your lovingkindness in the morning, for I completely trust in you. Cause me to know the way in which I should walk, for I lift up my soul to you.[8] Help me to walk in your ways at all times, dear Father.

Teach me to do your will, for you are my God. Your Spirit is so good to me. Lead me into the land of uprightness and obedience.[9]

Quicken me, O Lord God, for your name's sake. For your righteousness' sake, help me to keep my soul out of trouble.[10] Father, I want to experience the blessedness you promise to me, and I know that this will happen, as I walk in the light of your Word.[11] The entrance of your Word gives me light, Father,[12] for your Word is a lamp unto my feet and a light unto my path.[13]

Help me to experience the happiness you promise to all those who keep your testimonies and seek you with all their hearts.[14] It is my heart's desire to seek you at all times, Father, and to keep from all iniquity by walking in your ways.[15] Help me in this, Lord God.

You have commanded me to keep your precepts because you love me, and I will do so with your help.[16] Let my ways always be directed to keep your Word and your statutes, Father.[17] Then I will not be ashamed, because I will have continual respect unto all your commandments.[18]

Thank you for hearing and answering my prayer. In the name of your obedient Son, Jesus, I pray, Amen.[19]

References: *(1) Psalm 84:11; (2) Psalm 84:8; (3) Psalm 84:9; (4) Psalm 84:10; (5) Psalm 56:13; (6) Psalm 116:16; (7) Psalm 116:17; (8) Psalm 143:8; (9) Psalm 143:10; (10) Psalm 143:11; (11) Psalm 119:1; (12) Psalm 119:130; (13) Psalm 119:105; (14) Psalm 119:2; (15) Psalm 119:3; (16) Psalm 119:4; (17) Psalm 119:5; (18) Psalm 119:6; (19) John 16:23.*

39

Oppression

Prayer Purpose: To ask God to deliver you from all oppression in your life.

Key Scripture: *"Direct my steps by Your word, and let no iniquity have dominion over me. Redeem me from the oppression of man, that I may keep Your precepts"* (Ps. 119:133-134, NKJV).

Prayer: Father God, I ask you to help me to order my steps in your Word and to prevent iniquity and oppression from having any dominion over me. Deliver me from all forms of oppression, that I will be able to keep your precepts.[1]

The entrance of your words gives me light, Father, and it gives me understanding as well.[2] Make your face shine upon me, and teach me your statutes.[3]

Help me in this time of oppression, Lord God.[4] Set me in safety from the oppression of the enemy in my life.[5] Your words are as pure as silver that has been tried in a furnace and purified seven times.[6] Thank you for the power of your Word in my life.

I trust you, Father, to command your lovingkindness to me as I pray unto you.[7] You are my Rock, and I trust you to deliver me from the oppression of the enemy.[8] I know you will not forget my affliction and the oppression

I've been experiencing.[9] Arise and help me, Father God.[10]

Give ear to my prayer, O God, and do not hide yourself from my supplication.[11] Attend unto me, and hear me.[12] Deliver me completely from the oppression of the enemy and all wickedness.[13] Thank you for hearing and answering my prayer, dear God.[14]

I take refuge in you, Father. Thank you for being my refuge in times of trouble and oppression.[15] I know your name, and I put my trust in you, for I know you will never forsake me.[16] Thank you, God, for delivering me from all oppression.

In the glorious name of Jesus Christ I pray, Amen.[17]

References: *(1) Psalm 119:133-134; (2) Psalm 119:130; (3) Psalm 119:135; (4) Psalm 12:1; (5) Psalm 12:5; (6) Psalm 12:6; (7) Psalm 42:8; (8) Psalm 42:9; (9) Psalm 44:24; (10) Psalm 44:26; (11) Psalm 55:1; (12) Psalm 55:2; (13) Psalm 55:10-11; (14) Psalm 55:18; (15) Psalm 9:9; (16) Psalm 9:10; (17) John 15:16.*

40

Peace

Prayer Purpose: To thank God for His peace and to ask Him for help in maintaining the peace He gives to you.

Key Scripture: *"Great peace have those who love Your law, and nothing causes them to stumble"* (Ps. 119:165, NKJV).

Prayer: Heavenly Father, I love your Word, and I thank you for the great peace it imparts to me.[1] Thank you for putting gladness and peace in my heart. Because of your goodness to me, I will live and sleep in peace, and I know I will dwell safely and securely at all times.[2] Thank you, Lord God.

As I pray to you, I claim your promise that you will give both strength and peace to me.[3] Your peace is such a blessing to me, Father. Help me always to keep my tongue from evil and my lips from speaking guile.[4] With your help, I will depart from evil and do good. I will seek and pursue your peace at all times.[5]

Thank you for your promise which assures me that those who are meek shall inherit the earth and be able to delight themselves in the abundance of peace.[6] Father, I believe and receive this promise of abundant peace in my life right now. Thank you so much for providing this inheritance for me.

Thank you for speaking peace to me, Father,[7] and thank you for your salvation, which allows your righteousness and peace to kiss and meet each other in my life.[8] I receive your peace deep within me, as I pray.[9]

I praise you, O God, for you have strengthened my gates and blessed my family.[10] Thank you for the peace that surrounds me and the ways in which you are supplying all my needs.[11]

In the powerful name of Jesus I pray, Amen.[12]

References: (1) Psalm 119:165; (2) Psalm 4:7-8; (3) Psalm 29:11; (4) Psalm 34:13; (5) Psalm 34:14; (6) Psalm 37:11; (7) Psalm 85:8; (8) Psalm 85:9-10; (9) Psalm 122:8; (10) Psalm 147:13; (11) Psalm 147:14; (12) John 16:23.

41

Praising God

Prayer Purpose: To praise God for who He is and for all He has done for you.

Key Scripture: *"Praise the Lord! For it is good to sing praises to our God; for it is pleasant, and praise is beautiful"* (Ps. 147:1, NKJV).

Prayer: Father, I praise you for who you are and for all you've done for me. It is so good, pleasant, and beautiful to sing your praises.[1] I will ever tell my soul to praise you.[2] While I live I will praise you, Father; I will sing praises to you while I have my being.[3]

Thank you for the happiness that comes from having you, O God, as my help. All of my hope is in you.[4] I praise you and thank you for creating the universe and keeping your truth forever.[5]

I praise you, Father, for executing judgment for the oppressed, giving food to the hungry, loosing prisoners, opening blind eyes, lifting up those who are bowed down, loving the righteous, preserving strangers, and relieving the fatherless and widows.[6] I know you shall reign forever, O great King.[7]

Thank you, also, for healing the broken-hearted and binding up their wounds.[8] You are so great, Almighty God, and your power is glorious. Your understanding is infinite.[9] Thank you for lifting up the meek and casting the wicked down.[10]

For all these reasons and so many more, I sing unto you with thanksgiving.[11] I praise you, Lord God, both in your sanctuary and in the firmament of your power.[12]

I praise you for your mighty acts, according to your excellent greatness.[13] I praise you with music and song.[14] Thank you for the joy and freedom I experience as I praise you, Father.

In Jesus' name, Amen.[15]

References: (1) Psalm 147:1; (2) Psalm 146:1; (3) Psalm 146:2; (4) Psalm 146:5; (5) Psalm 146:6; (6) Psalm 146:7-9; (7) Psalm 146:10; (8) Psalm 147:3; (9) Psalm 147:4-5; (10) Psalm 147:6; (11) Psalm 147:7; (12) Psalm 150:1; (13) Psalm 150:2; (14) Psalm 150:3-6; (15) John 15:16.

42

Presence of God

Prayer Purpose: To thank God for the benefits you enjoy in His presence and to ask Him to help you dwell in His presence at all times.

Key Scripture: *"You will show me the path of life; in Your presence is fullness of joy; at Your right hand are pleasures forevermore"* (Ps. 16:11, NKJV).

Prayer: Heavenly Father, thank you for showing me the path of life and for letting me experience fullness of joy in your presence. At your right hand, I find pleasures forevermore.[1]

Oh, how great is your goodness, which you have provided for me and for all those who reverentially fear you and trust you.[2] Help me always to revere you and trust you. I believe and receive your promise that you will hide me in the secret of your presence, from the pride of man.[3]

Do not let me ever depart from your wonderful presence, Father.[4] I take great joy and pleasure from singing to you, Father, and making a joyful noise unto you, for you are the Rock of my salvation.[5]

I come before your presence with thanksgiving for all you've done for me, and I joyfully praise you with psalms,[6] for you are my great

194

God and you are a great King above all gods.[7] Thank you, Father, for being my God and King.

It is my desire, dear God, to dwell in your presence always.[8] O Lord God, you have searched me and known me.[9] You know when I sit down and when I get up, and you understand all my thoughts.[10] There is not a word on my tongue that you do not know.[11]

Thank you, Father, for being behind me, going before me, and laying your hand upon me.[12] Wherever I go, your Spirit is always present with me.[13]

No matter where I go, you are there, your hand is leading me, and your right hand is holding me up.[14] Thank you for all these blessings, dear God.

Search me, O God, and know my heart. Try me, and know my thoughts. See if there be any wicked way in me, and lead me in the everlasting way, as I enjoy your presence.[15]

In the lovely name of Jesus I pray, Amen.[16]

References: (1) Psalm 16:11; (2) Psalm 31:19; (3) Psalm 31:20; (4) Psalm 51:11; (5) Psalm 95:1; (6) Psalm 95:2; (7) Psalm 95:3; (8) Psalm 140:13; (9) Psalm 139:1; (10) Psalm 139:2; (11) Psalm 139:4; (12) Psalm 139:5; (13) Psalm 139:7-9; (14) Psalm 139:10; (15) Psalm 139:23-24; (16) John 16:23.

43

Refuge in God

Prayer Purpose: To honor God as your refuge and your strength and to thank Him for being the One to whom you can always go.

Key Scripture: *"God is our refuge and strength, a very present help in trouble. Therefore we will not fear, even though the earth be removed, and though the mountains be carried into the midst of the sea"* (Ps. 46:1-2, NKJV).

Prayer: Thank you, heavenly Father, for being my refuge and strength. It is so good to know that you are my very present help in times of trouble.[1]

Because these facts of my faith are true, I will not fear.[2] Thank you, Almighty God, for always being with me and being my refuge from the storms of life.[3]

As I take this moment now to be still and to meditate on your greatness, O God, I become greatly assured that you always will be my refuge.[4] Thank you, Father, for being my refuge and my fortress. You are my God, and I safely trust in you.[5]

As I wait silently upon you, I realize that all my expectation is from you, Father.[6] You only are my Rock and my salvation. You are my defense, and I shall not be moved.[7]

My salvation and my glory are in you, O God, for you are the Rock of my strength and my refuge.[8] With your help, I will trust in you at all times, and I will pour out my heart to you. Thank you so much for being my eternal refuge.[9]

Father God, you are my refuge and my portion in the land of the living.[10] In fact, I live in you. Be merciful to me, O God, for my soul trusts in you. I find my refuge in the shadow of your wings.[11] As I cry unto you, I realize that you perform all things well for me.[12] Thank you, Father.

My heart is fixed, O God. My heart is fixed.[13] I will ever sing and give praise to you, for you are my refuge and my safe place forever.

In the holy name of Jesus I pray, Amen.[14]

References: *(1) Psalm 46:1; (2) Psalm 45:2; (3) Psalm 46:7; (4) Psalm 46:11; (5) Psalm 91:2; (6) Psalm 62:5; (7) Psalm 62:6; (8) Psalm 62:7; (9) Psalm 62:8; (10) Psalm 142:5; (11) Psalm 57:1; (12) Psalm 57:2; (13) Psalm 57:7; (14) John 16:23.*

44

Satisfaction

Prayer Purpose: To thank God for satisfying your every need.

Key Scripture: *"Oh, that men would give thanks to the Lord for His goodness, and for His wonderful works to the children of men! For He satisfies the longing soul, and fills the hungry soul with goodness"* (Ps. 107:8-9, NKJV).

Prayer: Heavenly Father, thank you for your goodness and all the wonderful works you've done in my life. Truly, you have satisfied my longing soul and filled my hungry soul with goodness.[1]

Thank you for being my Shepherd; because this is so, I know I shall never need to suffer want or lack again.[2] Praise your mighty name!

How excellent is your lovingkindness, O Lord. I rejoice to know your great love for me, and I trust you fully, as I find my place of refuge in the shadow of your wings.[3]

Thank you for abundantly satisfying me and permitting me to drink from the river of your pleasures.[4] With you, dear Father, is the fountain of life, and in your light I am enlightened.[5] Thank you for satisfying each of these needs in my life.

Father, my soul blesses you, and all that is within me blesses your holy name.[6] I will never forget all your wonderful benefits to me.[7] Thank you for forgiving all my iniquities and healing all my diseases. Thank you for redeeming my life from destruction. I rejoice in the knowledge that you have crowned me with your lovingkindness and your tender mercies.[8]

Thank you for satisfying my mouth with good things, so that my youth is renewed like the eagle's.[9] As I pray, I believe and receive your promise to satisfy me and fulfill my desires.[10]

Thank you for being near to me, Father, as I call upon you in truth.[11] Knowing you as my God and King gives me great satisfaction in every area of my life. Thank you so much, dear God.

In Jesus' victorious name I pray, Amen.[12]

References: *(1) Psalm 107:8-9; (2) Psalm 23:1; (3) Psalm 36:7; (4) Psalm 36:8; (5) Psalm 36:9; (6) Psalm 103:1; (7) Psalm 103:2; (8) Psalm 103:3-4; (9) Psalm 103:5; (10) Psalm 145:19; (11) Psalm 145:18; (12) John 16:23.*

45

Seeking God

Prayer Purpose: To draw close to God and to ask for His help in seeking Him more fully.

Key Scripture: *"Glory in His holy name; let the hearts of those rejoice who seek the Lord! Seek the Lord, and His strength; seek His face evermore"* (Ps. 105:3-4, NKJV)!

Prayer: Lord God, thank you for making it possible for me to seek you. I glory in your holy name, and I greatly rejoice, as I seek you and your strength. Help me ever to remember to seek your face, dear Father.[1]

You are my God, and I will seek you early. My soul thirsts for you, and I long to see your power and glory.[2]

Because your lovingkindness is better than life to me, my lips shall praise you. Thus will I bless you while I live, and I will lift up my hands in your name.[3]

As the deer pants after the water brooks, my soul pants after you, O God.[4] Indeed, my soul thirsts for you, the living God.[5]

Father, I rejoice in you and give thanks unto you, as I call upon your name.[6] I will sing unto you and talk of all your wondrous works.[7]

I glory in your holy name, Father, and I greatly rejoice, as I seek you more fully.[8] With your help, mighty God, I will seek you, your face, and your strength forevermore.[9]

It is a blessing to seek you, Father. I love your salvation, and I want to magnify you with everything I do and say.[10] Thank you so much for being my help and my Deliverer,[11] and thank you for enabling me to find you each time I seek you.

Help me to seek you with my whole heart at all times, Father,[12] and do not let me wander from your commandments.[13] Thank you for your promise that those who seek you will not lack any good thing.[14]

I will set you always before me, Lord God. Because you are at my right hand, I shall not be moved.[15] Thank you for showing me the path of life. In your presence I have fullness of joy; at your right hand I have pleasures forevermore.[16]

In the glorious name of Jesus I pray, Amen.[17]

References: (1) Psalm 105:3-4; (2) Psalm 63:1-2; (3) Psalm 63:3-4; (4) Psalm 42:1; (5) Psalm 42:2; (6) Psalm 105:1; (7) Psalm 105:2; (8) Psalm 105:3; (9) Psalm 105:4; (10) Psalm 40:16; (11) Psalm 40:17; (12) Psalm 119:2; (13) Psalm 119:10; (14) Psalm 34:10; (15) Psalm 16:8; (16) Psalm 16:11; (17) John 16:23.

46

Serving God

Prayer Purpose: To seek God's help in enabling you to become more effective in your service to Him and others and to thank Him for the opportunities He gives to you, His servant.

Key Scripture: *"Make a joyful noise to the Lord, all you lands! Serve the Lord with gladness; come before His presence with singing. Know that the Lord, He is God; it is He who has made us, and not we ourselves; we are His people and the sheep of His pasture"* (Ps. 100:1-3, NKJV).

Prayer: Father God, you are my Lord and Creator. Therefore, I desire to serve you at all times. With this purpose in mind, I will joyfully praise you, and I choose to serve you with gladness. I come before your presence with singing, knowing that you are my Lord and my God.[1] Help me to serve you more fully, dear God.

I realize that serving you, Father, involves worshiping you. Therefore, I enter your gates with thanksgiving, and I go into your courts with praise. I rejoice as I give thanks to you and bless your name,[2] for I know how good you are to me.

Thank you for your everlasting mercy and truth.[3] I want to serve you always, Father, in mercy and in truth.

It is with reverential awe and devotion that I serve you, dear God.[4] I trust in you, for you are my God.[5] My times are in your hand.[6]

Make your face to shine upon me, as I endeavor to serve you more fully.[7] What a privilege it is to serve you, Almighty God.

As I serve you, Father, I want to shout for joy, for I am so glad to be your servant. It is my desire to magnify you through the opportunities for service that come my way. Thank you for taking pleasure in my prosperity.[8] Father, my tongue shall speak of your righteousness and praise at all times.[9]

O God, turn unto me, and have mercy upon me. Give me your strength, as I serve you.[10] Deal bountifully with me, Father, that I may live and keep your Word.[11] Open my eyes, that I may behold wondrous things out of your Word.[12]

Establish your Word unto me, as your servant, Father,[13] and let your mercies come unto me.[14]

I love serving you, and I ask you to open many doors of service for me. In the mighty name of Jesus I pray, Amen.[15]

References: (1) Psalm 100:1-3; (2) Psalm 100:4; (3) Psalm 100:5; (4) Psalm 2:11; (5) Psalm 31:14; (6) Psalm 31:15; (7) Psalm 31:16; (8) Psalm 35:27; (9) Psalm 35:28; (10) Psalm 86:16; (11) Psalm 119:17; (12) Psalm 119:18; (13) Psalm 119:38; (14) Psalm 119:41; (15) John 15:16.

47
Strength

Prayer Purpose: To ask God for His strength and to honor Him as the strength of your life.

Key Scripture: *"I will love thee, O Lord, my strength. The Lord is my rock, and my fortress, and my deliverer; my God, my strength, in whom I will trust; my buckler, and the horn of my salvation, and my high tower"* (Ps. 18:1-2).

Prayer: Dear Father, my strength, I love you. You truly are my Rock, my fortress, my Deliverer, my God, my strength, my buckler, the horn of my salvation, and my high tower. Thank you so much for being all these things for me. I trust in you with all my heart.[1]

Strengthen me, Father, as I wait upon you, for I realize that it is you who girds me with strength, and you make my way perfect, as well.[2] Thank you, Father, for all the promises of your Word. I need your strength, so please strengthen me according to your Word.[3]

As I wait upon you, I realize you are strengthening my heart.[4] Thank you, Father, for hearing and answering my prayer for strength.

Let the words of my mouth and the meditations of my heart always be acceptable in your sight, O Lord God, my strength and my

Redeemer.[5] Thank you for being the strength of my life, Father.

Knowing this truly keeps me from fear.[6] You, Father God, are my refuge and strength at all times. Indeed, you are a very present help to me.[7] Thank you so much.

I rejoice to know that you, Father, are the strength of my heart and my portion forever.[8] Therefore, I will go forth in your strength from this time forward.[9]

Blessed are you, O Lord God, my strength, for you have taught my hands to war and my fingers to fight.[10]

You are my goodness, my fortress, my high tower, my Deliverer, and my strength, Father, and I place all my trust in you.[11] Thank you for hearing and answering my prayer for greater strength. I receive your strength into my life right now.

In the strong name of Jesus I pray, Amen.[12]

References: (1) Psalm 18:1-2; (2) Psalm 18:32; (3) Psalm 119:28; (4) Psalm 27:14; (5) Psalm 19:14; (6) Psalm 27:1; (7) Psalm 46:1; (8) Psalm 73:26; (9) Psalm 71:16; (10) Psalm 144:1; (11) Psalm 144:2; (12) John 16:23.

48

Teaching

Prayer Purpose: To ask God to teach you His ways and to seek His help in teaching others.

Key Scripture: *"Show me Your ways, O Lord; teach me Your paths. Lead me in Your truth and teach me, for You are the God of my salvation; on You I wait all the day"* (Ps. 25:4-5, NKJV).

Prayer: Father God, show me your ways, and teach me your paths. Lead me in your truth, and teach me, for you are the God of my salvation, and I wait on you all day long.[1]

Thank you for your tender mercies and lovingkindesses, which are at work in my life.[2] You are so good and upright, Lord God, and I want to be more like you. Therefore, I ask you to teach me your ways.[3]

Help me to walk in meekness and to be teachable, because I know these are qualities you desire to develop in me, as you teach me your ways.[4] Thank you, Father.

Teach me your way, O Lord God, and lead me in a plain path.[5] I believe and receive your promise that tells me you will instruct and teach me in the way in which I should go, and you will guide me with your eye.[6]

Teach me your way, O Lord God, for I want to walk in your truth at all times. Unite my heart to reverence you.[7] I ask you, Father, to teach me to do your will, for you are my God, and your Spirit is good.

Lead me into the land of uprightness.[8] Blessed are you, O God; teach me your statutes.[9] Help me to understand the way of your statutes, that I may talk to others of your wondrous works.[10]

Teach me good judgment and knowledge, for I believe your Word and all the commandments it contains.[11] How sweet are your words to me, Father, for through them I gain spiritual understanding.[12]

Teach me through your Word, for it truly is a lamp unto my feet and a light unto my path, and I want always to walk in the light it provides for me.[13] Thank you for teaching your ways to me.

In the name of Jesus I pray, Amen.[14]

References: *(1) Psalm 25:4-5; (2) Psalm 25:6; (3) Psalm 25:8; (4) Psalm 25:9; (5) Psalm 27:11; (6) Psalm 32:8; (7) Psalm 86:11; (8) Psalm 143:10; (9) Psalm 119:12; (10) Psalm 119:27; (11) Psalm 119:66; (12) Psalm 119:103; (13) Psalm 119:105; (14) John 15:16.*

49

Thanksgiving to God

Prayer Purpose: To express your gratitude to God for all He has done for you.

Key Scripture: *"Offer to God thanksgiving, and pay your vows to the Most High. Call upon Me in the day of trouble; I will deliver you, and you shall glorify Me"* (Ps. 50:14-15, NKJV).

Prayer: O God, my Father, I thank you so much for everything you've done for me. Thanks, also, for your wonderful invitation to call upon you in times of trouble, so I can be delivered and glorify you.[1]

It is my desire to glorify you always, and it is my joy, Father, to praise your name with a song and to magnify you with thanksgiving.[2]

I come before your presence with thanksgiving, and I make a joyful noise to you with psalms, for you are my great God, and you are the great King above all gods.[3] Father, I'm so thankful that I know you.

Dear Lord God, as I enter your gates with thanksgiving and go into your courts with praise, my heart soars, and I desire to bless your name, for I know how good you are. I'm so thankful to know that your mercy and truth will endure throughout all generations.[4]

Thank you for being my living God and my Rock; it is my desire to exalt you, because you are the God of my salvation.[5]

Thank you for your deliverance in my life, Father.[6] Knowing how you've helped me in so many ways, I will ever give thanks to you and sing praises to your name.[7]

Thank you, Father. It is so good to give thanks to you and to sing praises to your name, O Most High.[8] Help me to show forth your lovingkindness in the morning and your faithfulness every night.[9]

Lord God, you have made me glad, and I will ever triumph in the works of your hands.[10] How great are your works, and your thoughts are very deep.[11] Thank you, Father, for all you have done and for revealing your thoughts to me.

I give thanks to you, for you are good and your mercy endures forever.[12] I give thanks to you, because you do great wonders.[13]

By your wisdom you created the universe,[14] and you have redeemed me from all enemies.[15] Thank you, Father, for all the wonderful things you've done for me.

In Jesus' precious name I pray, Amen.[16]

References: (1) Psalm 50:14-15; (2) Psalm 69:30; (3) Psalm 95:2-3; (4) Psalm 100:4-5; (5) Psalm 18:46; (6) Psalm 18:48; (7) Psalm 18:49; (8) Psalm 92:1; (9) Psalm 92:2; (10) Psalm 92:4; (11) Psalm 92:5; (12) Psalm 136:1; (13) Psalm 136:4; (14) Psalm 136:5-9; (15) Psalm 136:24; (16) John 16:23.

50

Trials, Tribulations, and Trouble

Prayer Purpose: To ask God to help you during times of trial, tribulation, and trouble.

Key Scripture: *"The Lord also will be a refuge for the oppressed, a refuge in times of trouble. And those who know Your name will put their trust in You; For You, Lord, have not forsaken those who seek You"* (Ps. 9:9-10, NKJV).

Prayer: Father God, during this time of trouble in my life I turn to you, because I know you are my refuge, and I put my trust in you. I know you will not forsake me.[1]

Thank you for all the promises of your Word. Be not far from me, Father, for trouble is near.[2] Hide me in the safe place of your pavilion, and set me high upon a rock.[3] Thank you for hearing and answering my prayer.

I believe and receive your promise that you will preserve me from trouble and you will surround me with songs of deliverance, for you are my hiding place.[4]

Thank you, Father, for being my strength during this time of trouble.[5] I know you will help me and deliver me, because I trust in you.[6]

Thank you for always being my refuge and strength, Father, and for always being a very present help to me when I am in trouble.[7]

Therefore, I will not fear the current tribulations and troubles I am facing.[8] Thank you, Father.

I praise you so much for inviting me to call upon you in times of trouble. I do so now, Lord God, and I know you will deliver me. It is my desire to glorify you at all times.[9]

Give me help in this time of trial, Father,[10] for I know that I shall do valiantly through you and your help.[11]

I set my love upon you, Father, and I know you will deliver me.[12] Thank you so much for all the promises of your Word. Set me on high, I ask, because I know your name.[13]

As I call upon you, I believe I am receiving your answer. Thank you for being with me, Father, and for delivering me from trouble and honoring me.[14] I love you so much, dear God.

In the loving name of Jesus I pray, Amen.[15]

References: (1) Psalm 9:9-10; (2) Psalm 22:11; (3) Psalm 27:5; (4) Psalm 32:7; (5) Psalm 37:39; (6) Psalm 37:40; (7) Psalm 46:1; (8) Psalm 46:2; (9) Psalm 50:15; (10) Psalm 60:11; (11) Psalm 60:12; (12) Psalm 91:14; (13) Psalm 91:14; (14) Psalm 91:15; (15) John 15:16.

51

Trusting God

Prayer Purpose: To ask God to help you trust Him and His Word more fully.

Key Scripture: *"I will love thee, O Lord, my strength. The Lord is my rock, and my fortress, and my deliverer; my God, my strength, in whom I will trust; my buckler, and the horn of my salvation, and my high tower"* (Ps. 18:1-2).

Prayer: O Lord God, my strength, I love you. Thank you for being my Rock, my fortress, my Deliverer, my God, my strength, my buckler, the horn of my salvation, and my high tower. I trust in you, Father, and I ask you to help me to trust you more fully at all times.[1]

Some place their trust in chariots and some in horses, but I will remember your name, Lord God, and I will trust in you.[2]

I lift up my soul to you, Father, and I trust in you. Please don't ever let me be ashamed, and don't let my enemies ever triumph over me.[3] I place all my trust in you, Lord God, and I ask you to deliver me in your righteousness.[4]

Bow down your ear to me, and deliver me speedily. Be my strong Rock and a house of defense for me.[5] Thank you for being my Rock and my fortress. For your name's sake, lead me and guide me.[6]

As I learn to trust in you more fully, Father, I ask for your help in doing good.[7]

I will delight myself in you at all times, and, as I do so, I know you will give me the desires of my heart.[8]

Thank you for all the wonderful promises of your Word. Father, I commit my way to you, as I grow in my ability to trust in you, and I know you will hear and answer my prayer.[9] Thank you so much.

Help me to dwell in your secret place, Most High God, and to abide under your shadow.[10] You are my refuge and my fortress. Thank you for being my God. I place all my trust in you.[11]

Thank you for your Word, Father. I trust in your Word, and I delight myself in it, for I love your Word.[12] Thank you for hearing and answering my prayer by helping me to trust you more fully.

In Jesus' great name I pray, Amen.[13]

References: *(1) Psalm 18:1-2; (2) Psalm 20:7; (3) Psalm 25:1-2; (4) Psalm 31:1; (5) Psalm 31:2; (6) Psalm 31:3; (7) Psalm 37:3; (8) Psalm 37:4; (9) Psalm 37:5; (10) Psalm 91:1; (11) Psalm 91:2; (12) Psalm 119:42; (13) John 16:23.*

52

Truth

Prayer Purpose: To thank God for the truth of His Word and to ask Him to help you walk in truth at all times.

Key Scripture: *"Lead me in Your truth and teach me, for You are the God of my salvation; on You I wait all the day"* (Ps. 25:5, NKJV).

Prayer: Father God, lead me in your truth and teach me, as I wait on you in prayer.[1] Show me your ways, O God, and teach me your paths.[2]

I thank you that you have redeemed me, O Lord of truth,[3] and that all of your paths are paved with mercy and truth.[4] Examine me, O God, and prove me,[5] for your lovingkindness is before my eyes, and I desire to walk in your truth.[6]

O God, my Father, send out your light and your truth. Let them lead me.[7] For your Word tells me that those that abide in your presence must walk in integrity, work righteousness, and speak truth in their hearts.[8] Because I know you desire truth to be found in my inward parts, I ask you to make me to know your wisdom in my heart of hearts.[9]

You are so great, dear Father, and you do so many wondrous things.[10] Thank you for all you are doing in my life.

Teach me your way, O Lord God, as I endeavor to walk in your truth. Unite my heart to reverence you at all times, I pray.[11] How I thank you that you are full of compassion, gracious, longsuffering, and abundant in both mercy and truth.[12]

Father, let your lovingkindness and your truth continually preserve me.[13] I take your truth as my shield and buckler.[14] I have chosen the way of your truth, O God. I have laid your judgments before me, and I will cling to your testimonies.[15]

Dear God, I will hide your Word in my heart, that I might not sin against you.[16] The entrance of your Word enlightens me and gives me understanding.[17] I trust completely in your Word of truth.[18]

Thank you for being near to me, Father, and for the fact that all your commandments are truth.[19] Your Word is a lamp unto my feet and a light unto my path. Help me to walk in the light of your Word from this time forward.[20]

Lord God, you are good! Your mercy is everlasting, and your truth endures to all generations.[21] Hallelujah!

In Jesus' wonderful name I pray, Amen.[22]

References: *(1) Psalm 25:5; (2) Psalm 25:4; (3) Psalm 31:5; (4) Psalm 25:10; (5) Psalm 26:2; (6) Psalm 26:3; (7) Psalm 43:3; (8) Psalm 15:1-2; (9) Psalm 51:6-7; (10) Psalm 86:10; (11) Psalm 86:11; (12) Psalm 86:15; (13) Psalm 40:11; (14) Psalm 91:4; (15) Psalm 119:30-31; (16) Psalm 119:11; (17) Psalm 119:130; (18) Psalm 119:42; (19) Psalm 119:151; (20) Psalm 119:105; (21) Psalm 100:5; (22) John 15:16.*

53

Understanding

Prayer Purpose: To ask God for greater spiritual understanding and to thank Him for the understanding He has imparted to you.

Key Scripture: *"My mouth shall speak of wisdom; and the meditation of my heart shall be of understanding"* (Ps. 49:3).

Prayer: O God, my heavenly Father, please give me your wisdom, that I will be able to proclaim it to others, and the meditations of my heart will be filled with spiritual understanding.[1]

Help me to be faithful in keeping all your commandments, Lord God, because I realize this will lead me into greater realms of spiritual understanding.[2]

Teach me, O Lord God, the way of your statutes, and I will always endeavor to keep them.[3] Give me understanding, that I would be able to keep your law and observe it with all my heart.[4]

Help me to proceed in the path of your commandments, for I find my delight in your Word.[5]

Father, because I know your hands have made me and fashioned me, I look to you, my Creator, for the understanding I need to learn and follow your commandments and all of your ways.[6]

My hope, dear God, is in your Word.[7] Thank you for giving me greater spiritual understanding through your precious Word.[8]

How thankful I am for your Word, which is a lamp unto my feet and a light unto my path.[9] Help me, Father God, to walk in the light of your Word and the understanding it gives to me at all times.

Father, I am your servant. Give me understanding, that I may always know your testimonies and truths.[10]

The entrance of your Word gives light and understanding to me.[11] Thank you, Father. Give me greater understanding, Lord God, that I might live more fully and abundantly in you.[12]

Father, I love your precepts. Quicken me according to your lovingkindness. Your Word is true from the beginning, and every one of its judgments endure forever. My heart stands in awe of your Word, and I greatly rejoice in your Word.[13]

Indeed I love your Word, and this gives me great peace. Let my cry come before you, Father, and give me understanding according to your Word.[14]

As you give me understanding according to your Word, I will grow greatly determined in my heart to praise you, serve you, love you, and obey you.[15] Help me, Father.

Thank you for hearing and answering my prayer. In Jesus' name I pray, Amen.[16]

References: (1) *Psalm 49:3; (2) Psalm 111:10; (3) Psalm 119:33; (4) Psalm 119:34; (5) Psalm 119:35; (6) Psalm 119:73; (7) Psalm 119:74; (8) Psalm 119:104; (9) Psalm 119:105; (10) Psalm 119:125; (11) Psalm 119:130; (12) Psalm 119:144; (13) Psalm 119:159-162; (14) Psalm 119:163-169; (15) Psalm 119:169; (16) John 16:23.*

54

Waiting on God

Prayer Purpose: To spend time before the Lord in prayer and worship and to ask Him to help you, as you wait on Him.

Key Scripture: *"To You, O Lord, I lift up my soul. O my God, I trust in You; let me not be ashamed; let not my enemies triumph over me....Show me Your ways, O Lord; teach me Your paths. Lead me in Your truth and teach me, for You are the God of my salvation; on You I wait all the day"* (Ps. 25:1-5, NKJV).

Prayer: O God of my salvation, I lift up my soul to you, and I trust in you. Let me not be ashamed, and do not let my enemies triumph over me. Show me your ways, Lord God, and teach me your paths. Lead me in your truth, and teach me. You are the God of my salvation. I wait before you with expectant hope all the day long.[1] Let integrity and uprightness preserve me, as I wait on you.[2]

Father God, help me to remember to wait on you at all times and to be of good courage, for I know that, as I do these things, you will strengthen my heart.[3] Thank you, Father, for this precious promise from your Word.

Help me to rest in you, Lord God, and to wait patiently for you.[4] Teach me how to wait on you, Father, and to keep your ways.[5]

Thank you for making me flourish like a green olive tree in your house, dear God. I trust in your mercy, and I will praise you forever. Be near to me, as I wait on you in prayer.[6] Help me ever to remember to wait only upon you, Father, for all of my expectation is from you.

Father, you truly are my Rock, my salvation, and my defense.[7] Thank you for being so good to me, for in you I find my salvation and my glory, and I rejoice to know that you are the Rock of my strength and my refuge.[8] Thank you, Lord God.

I love you, Father, as I wait for you and hope in your Word.[9] Waiting patiently for you, I realize you are inclining unto me and hearing my cry.[10]

Thank you for hearing and answering my prayer, dear God. As I praise you, I wait for you, for you are the One who hears and answers prayer.[11] As I still my heart before you, I know that you alone are my God.[12] In your presence I find fullness of joy and pleasures forevermore.[13]

I experience your peace, dear Father, as I wait on you.[14] In Jesus' blessed name I pray, Amen.[15]

References: *(1) Psalm 25:1-5; (2) Psalm 25:21; (3) Psalm 27:14; (4) Psalm 37:7; (5) Psalm 37:34; (6) Psalm 52:8-9; (7) Psalm 62:6; (8) Psalm 62:7; (9) Psalm 130:5; (10) Psalm 40:1; (11) Psalm 65:1-2; (12) Psalm 46:10; (13) Psalm 16:11; (14) Psalm 29:11; (15) John 15:16.*

55

Wisdom

Prayer Purpose: To ask for God's wisdom and to thank Him for the wisdom He has imparted to you.

Key Scripture: *"My mouth shall speak of wisdom; and the meditation of my heart shall be of understanding"* (Ps. 49:3).

Prayer: Father God, I ask you for greater wisdom, that my mouth may proclaim it to others and my heart shall meditate on the understanding it imparts to me.[1] Let your truth fill my spirit, Father, and let me know your wisdom deep within.[2]

Teach me to number my days, that I will apply my heart to the wisdom you impart to me.[3] Thank you for wisdom, Father.

I bless you for the wisdom your Word imparts to me. Help me always to remember to hide your Word in my heart, that I might not sin against you.[4]

Deal bountifully with me, that I may live and keep your Word.[5] Open my eyes, Father, that I may behold the wondrous wisdom of your Word.[6]

Teach me, O Lord God, the way of your statutes, and help me to keep them throughout my life.[7] Give me wisdom and understanding from your Word, and I will always endeavor to walk in your wisdom.[8] I need your wisdom, dear God.

Your Word truly is a lamp unto my feet and a light unto my path.[9] Help me to walk in its light each day. Your Word shows me that your mercy endures forever, and you do great wonders. Indeed, you made the heavens through your wisdom.[10]

This is wonderful knowledge to me, Father, and it causes me to experience the wisdom that comes from reverential awe of you.[11]

Thank you for hearing and answering my prayer for greater wisdom. In Jesus' holy name I pray, Amen.[12]

References: (1) Psalm 49:3; (2) Psalm 51:6; (3) Psalm 90:12; (4) Psalm 119:11; (5) Psalm 119:17; (6) Psalm 119:18; (7) Psalm 119:33; (8) Psalm 119:34; (9) Psalm 119:105; (10) Psalm 136:1-5; (11) Psalm 111:10; (12) John 16:23.

56

Worship

Prayer Purpose: To worship the Lord God and to ask Him to teach you how to worship Him more fully.

Key Scripture: *"Give unto the Lord the glory due unto his name: bring an offering, and come into his courts. O worship the Lord in the beauty of holiness: fear before him, all the earth"* (Ps. 96:8-9).

Prayer: Father God, I desire to worship you in the beauty of holiness, so I can give unto you the glory that is due to your name.[1]

Teach me to worship you in spirit, in truth, and in the beauty of holiness. It is a good thing to give thanks unto you and to sing praise to your name, O Most High.[2] Help me to show forth your lovingkindness in the morning and your faithfulness every night.[3]

You are my God, and I desire to worship you fully at all times.[4] Show me how to do so, Father. You are my dwelling place.[5]

Before the mountains and all the earth were created, even from everlasting to everlasting, you were, are, and will always be the Lord God of the universe.[6] I worship you, Father.

Thank you for being my great God and a great King above all gods.[7] The strength of the hills is yours, O Father.[8]

You made the sea, and it is yours; your hands formed the dry land as well.[9] For all these reasons and so many more, I worship and bow down in your presence. I kneel before you, Lord God, my Creator.[10]

My God and King, you rule and reign over all your creation.[11] Thank you for your glory and your power.[12] It is such a delight for me to exalt you, Lord God, and to worship at your footstool, for you are holy.[13] In your presence I experience fullness of joy and pleasures forevermore.[14]

O Lord, my God, I will bless you and worship you, for you are very great. You are clothed with honor and majesty.[15] O Lord, how many are your wonderful works! In wisdom you have made them all; the earth is full of your riches.[16]

Your glory shall endure forever. I will sing unto you, Lord God, for as long as I live. I will sing praise to you all my life. My meditation of you is always sweet when I worship you.[17]

Thank you for hearing and answering my prayer, as I exalt you through worship.[18] Father God, you are holy, and I deeply desire to worship you in the beauty of holiness.[19]

In Jesus' name, Amen.[20]

References: (1) Psalm 29:2; (2) Psalm 92:1; (3) Psalm 92:2; (4) Psalm 45:11; (5) Psalm 90:1; (6) Psalm 90:2; (7) Psalm 95:3; (8) Psalm 95:4; (9) Psalm 95:5; (10) Psalm 95:6; (11) Psalm 99:1; (12) Psalm 99:2-3; (13) Psalm 99:5; (14) Psalm 16:11; (15) Psalm 104:1; (16) Psalm 104:24; (17) Psalm 104:31-34; (18) Psalm 99:9; (19) Psalm 96:9; (20) John 15:16.

Psalms of Power

Prayers

of

Purpose

We trust that, by now, you have experienced the great power of the Psalms and have enjoyed a multitude of benefits that come from praying the Psalms.

In chapter five, "Topical Prayers," you found fifty-six prayers that were composed from hundreds of different verses in the Book of Psalms. By weaving these verses together, we were able to compose prayers that address major themes and topics from a personal perspective, prayers for you to use as springboards in your own prayer life.

The present chapter, "Psalms of Power — Prayers of Purpose," takes an approach that is somewhat different from the other two. In this chapter you will be encouraged to personalize and pray paraphrases of certain major, well-known Psalms.

We have selected key Psalms that lend themselves particularly well to this approach. Many of these Psalms were not originally written as prayers, but, as you will soon discover, they readily adapt themselves to the life of prayer in surprisingly powerful ways. In many cases, we have adapted and paraphrased particular Psalms in their entirety.

Use the following prayers, therefore, to "prime the pump" in your own devotional life by using them as tools for personal prayer, study, and Bible meditation. Let God speak to you through His Word, as you employ this approach in your personal prayer life. These Psalms of power used as prayers of purpose will give you new perspectives on the important truths of God's Word.

Steps to Take

As you prepare to pray the following Psalms, we encourage you to take the following steps:

1. Read the entire passage from the King James Version of the Holy Bible. Then compare and contrast this translation of the particular Psalm with other versions and paraphrases, such as The New King James Version, the New International Version, the Amplified Bible, or other versions. Take notes on the main points you discover.

2. Spend some time meditating on the passage. Let its truths sink deep into your spirit. Ponder its main points, and reflect on their significance in your own life. Ask God to open the eyes of your understanding and to speak to your heart.

3. Personalize the passage. Let each verse apply to your personal life by seeing if it contains any promises for

you to claim, errors for you to avoid, examples for you to follow, or commands for you to obey. As you do this, remember that God's Word is "...given by inspiration of God, and is profitable for doctrine, for reproof, for correction, for instruction in righteousness, that the man of God may be complete, thoroughly equipped for every good work" (2 Tim. 3:16, NKJV).

4. Turn the passage into a prayer. Though we have already done this step for you, God may give you additional insights that you may wish to incorporate into your prayers. The important thing is to remember that you are offering the passage back to God as a prayer, and, as you do this, God promises, "...that He hears us, whatever we ask, [and] we know that we have the petitions that we have asked of Him" (1 John 5:15, NKJV). We know this is true, because when we pray God's Word, we pray His will, and He always honors His Word.

5. Pray, pray, pray. Prayer is a two-way communication between you and God. He promises to hear you when you pray according to His will. By praying these Psalms you are praying

His will for your life. In so doing, your faith will be strengthened and you will receive the wonderful things God has in store for you.

As you pray, keep these words of Jesus in mind: "And whatever you ask in My name, that I will do, that the Father may be glorified in the Son. If you ask anything in My name, I will do it" (John 14:13-14, NKJV).

1

Psalm 1 – Loving God's Word

Thoughts to Ponder Before You Pray: Meditating on the Word of God is one of life's greatest privileges. Such meditation increases your faith. Paul writes, "So then faith comes by hearing, and hearing by the word of God" (Rom. 10:17, NKJV).

God promises prosperity, fruitfulness, happiness, and stability to you as a result of meditating on His Word. By praying the Word, you are letting Bible meditation have its powerful effects in your life.

Prayer: Thank you, Father, for the blessedness I enjoy when I avoid ungodly counsel, do not stand in the path of sinners, and do not sit in the seat of scorners.

Help me always to avoid such errors in my life, for my delight is in your Word, and I choose to meditate therein both night and day. Help me to do so, Father, and to enjoy the happiness this brings to me.

Your wonderful Word is filled with promises for me to claim, and one of these tells me that, as I meditate upon your Word, you will cause me to be like a tree that is planted by the rivers of water.

Thank you, Father, for this promise and for promising me that I will be fruitful as well. It blesses me to know that, as a result of Bible meditation, my leaf shall not wither, and whatever I do shall prosper. Thank you, Father.

Your Word tells me, also, that the ungodly are not so, but are like the chaff driven away by the wind. Therefore, the ungodly shall not stand in the judgment, and sinners will not stand in the congregation of the righteous.

Thank you, Father, for showing me that you know the way of the righteous, but the way of the ungodly shall perish. Help me always to walk in your righteousness and godliness.

In Jesus' name I pray, Amen.

2

Psalm 5 – Confidence in God

Thoughts to Ponder Before You Pray: God loves you and is merciful to you. He wants you to pray to Him both night and day. God wants you to worship Him in spirit and in truth.

Jesus said, "But the hour is coming, and now is, when the true worshipers will worship the Father in spirit and truth; for the Father is seeking such to worship Him. God is Spirit, and those who worship Him must worship in spirit and truth" (John 4:23-24, NKJV).

As you pray the following Psalm, let a spirit of worship come over you. Begin to praise God for all He has done for you and to worship Him for who He is, your Father who loves you with an everlasting love.

As a result of such vital praying, your confidence and trust in God will grow, and you will experience the favor of your heavenly Father.

Prayer: Lord God, give ear to my words and consider my meditation. Give heed to the voice of my cry, my King and my God, for I am praying to you. You shall hear my voice in the morning, dear Father, because I will direct my prayer to you in the morning, and I will always look up to you.

I thank you that you do not ever take pleasure in wickedness, and evil does not dwell with you. Your Word assures me, Father, that the boastful will not stand in your sight, and you hate all workers of iniquity.

I know you will deal with those who speak falsehood, because you abhor bloodthirsty and deceitful people, and so do I. Keep me from ever being boastful or deceitful, dear God.

It gives me great joy, Father God, to come into your house in the multitude of your mercies. In reverential awe, I will worship toward your holy temple and take joy in your presence. Lead me, O Lord God, in your righteousness, and make your way straight before my face.

People who do not know you, have no faithfulness in their mouths. Their throats are open tombs, and they flatter with their tongues. I never want to be like them, Father. I ask you to deal with them in your own way.

However, as one of those who rejoice in you, I ask you to help me trust you more and more. Let me ever shout for joy, because I know you will always defend me. Thank you, Father.

I love your name, and I am joyful in you, for I know that you, Lord God, will bless me, and you will surround me with favor as with a shield.

In Jesus' name I pray, Amen.

3

Psalm 9 – A Victorious Song of Praise

Thoughts to Ponder Before You Pray: God is the King of His universe — a universe that He created. He it is that fights many battles for us and enables us to be victorious over the enemy of our souls and all other enemies.

It is appropriate for us to thank Him for giving us the victory, even in advance, for God's Word assures us, "Yet in all these things we are more than conquerors through Him who loved us" (Rom. 8:37, NKJV).

Prayer: I will praise you, O Lord God, with my whole heart. I will tell of all your marvelous works, and I will be glad and rejoice in you.

I will sing praise to your name, O Most High. When my enemies retreat, I know they shall fall in your presence, for you always maintain my right and my cause. Thank you, Father.

From your throne, mighty King, you judge in righteousness. You have rebuked the nations, destroyed the wicked, and blotted out their names forevermore. Even their memory has perished.

Unlike them, however, you, Lord God, shall endure forever. Thank you for preparing your throne for judgment, so you will judge the world in righteousness and administer judgment for all people in uprightness. Thank you, Father.

I praise you for the fact that you are always a refuge for the oppressed, and a refuge for me in times of trouble. I know your name, Lord God, and I place all my trust in you, for you, my Father, have never forsaken me, or anyone else who seeks you.

Therefore, I sing praises to you, and I ask you to help me to declare your deeds among the people. I know you will never forget the cries of the humble. Keep me humble, Father.

Have mercy on me, Lord God. Lift me up, that I may proclaim your praise everywhere I go. I greatly rejoice in the salvation you've given to me.

Deal with the wicked, Father, and all the nations that forget you. I thank you so much that you will not forget the needy, and the expectation of the poor shall not perish forever.

Meet the needs of the poor, and arise, O Lord God. Don't let mankind prevail. Let the nations be judged in your sight. Reveal to the leaders of this world that they are but men, and they need you desperately.

In the mighty name of Jesus I pray, Amen.

4

Psalm 15 – Living Righteously

Thoughts to Ponder Before You Pray: Thomas Jefferson said that this Psalm gives us a true picture of a gentleman. Keep this in mind as you pray these words of truth, and remember that Jesus Christ, the ultimate Gentleman, is your righteousness.

Paul wrote, "But of him are ye in Christ Jesus, who of God is made unto us wisdom, and righteousness, and sanctification, and redemption" (1 Cor. 1:30).

It is the righteousness of Christ, which has been imputed to you, that enables you to live righteously, "For he hath made him to be sin for us, who knew no sin; that we might be made the righteousness of God in him" (2 Cor. 5:21).

Prayer: Lord God, who shall abide in your tabernacle? Who shall dwell in your holy hill? It is clear to me, Father, that only righteous people shall be able to have such special spiritual privileges.

Therefore, I ask you to help me walk in the righteousness you have provided for me at all times. Help me to walk uprightly, to work righteousness in all that I do, and to speak the truth in and from my heart.

Keep me from ever using my tongue to engage in backbiting. I never want to do evil to my neighbor, or to take up a reproach against my friends. Help me, Father. Thank you for your promise to honor me, as I trust in you.

Dear God, with your help, I will not lend money at usury nor take a bribe against the innocent. Help me to keep from all forms of evil and to walk in righteousness at all times. I believe and receive your promise that I shall not be moved.

In Jesus' righteous name I pray, Amen.

5

Psalm 18 – A Hymn of Thanksgiving

Thoughts to Ponder Before You Pray: This Psalm expresses David's deep gratitude to God for allowing him to ascend to the throne of Israel after so many years of fleeing from Saul and others. In this lovely hymn, the king gives God the glory for everything, and this is a great example for every believer to follow.

Prayer: I will love you, O Lord God, my strength, for you are my Rock, my fortress, my Deliverer, my strength, my shield, the horn of my salvation, and my stronghold. I put all my trust in you, Father.

I call upon you, because you are so worthy to be praised, and I know I shall be saved from all enemies. Thank you, Father.

Though the pangs of death surrounded me, the floods of ungodliness threatened to overwhelm me, the sorrows of Sheol surrounded me, and the snares of death confronted me, I called upon you in my distress. I cried out to you, Lord God, and you heard my voice from your temple, and my cry came before you. Thank you for hearing and answering my prayer.

Thank you for drawing me out of so many turbulent waters and for delivering me from my strong enemy, from those who hated me, for they were too strong for me. Though they confronted me in the day of my calamity, you, Lord God, were my strong support.

Thank you for bringing me out of those difficulties and into a broad place. I rejoice when I realize how completely you delivered me. Thank you, Father, for taking such delight in me.

I praise you, Lord God, for rewarding me according to the righteousness you've imparted to me; according to the cleanness of my hands you have recompensed me. For I have kept your ways and have not departed from you. All of your judgments are before me, and I seek your help, that I would never put them away from me.

Thank you for making me blameless before you and helping me keep myself free from all iniquity. I am so thrilled to know that you always show yourself merciful to the merciful, blameless to the blameless, and pure to the pure. Help me, Father, to walk in mercy, blamelessness, and purity at all times.

Father, I believe and receive your promise that you will light my lamp and enlighten my darkness. By you, I can run through a troop and leap over a wall. Dear God, I realize that your way is perfect and your Word is proven.

Thank you for being a shield to me at all times, as I trust in you.

You are my God and my Lord. You are my Rock. It is you who arms me with strength and makes my way perfect. Thank you, Father, for making my feet like the feet of a deer and for setting me in high places. Thank you for teaching my hands to war, so my arms can bend a bow of bronze.

Thank you for giving me the shield of your salvation. Your right hand has held me up, and your gentleness has made me great. Thank you for enlarging my path under me, so my feet would not slip.

Father God, you have armed me with strength for the battle, and you have subdued under me those who rose up against me. Thank you, Father.

You are alive, O God! Blessed are you, my Rock! I want you, the God of my salvation, ever to be exalted, for I know it is you who avenges me and subdues all enemies under me.

Thank you, again, for delivering me from my enemies and lifting me up above those who rise against me. Father, I praise you for delivering me from all violence and violent people.

Therefore, I give thanks to you, O Lord God, and I sing praises to your name. I rejoice in the great deliverance you give to me and the wonderful mercy you show to my descendants and me.

In Jesus' victorious name I pray, Amen.

6

Psalm 19 – The Word of God

Thoughts to Ponder Before You Pray: In this Psalm of David, we learn that God's Word is perfect, pure, true, and sweeter than honey. This is a Psalm that glorifies God's creation and exalts His Word.

Psalm 19 concludes with a very earnest and stirring prayer for protection from sin and a plea for spiritual purity.

Prayer: Father God, the heavens declare you glory, and the firmament shows forth your handiwork. Your Word is perfect; it converts the soul. Your testimony is sure; it gives wisdom to the simple, who approach you in child-like faith.

Lord, your statutes are righteous, and they bring rejoicing to my heart. Your commandment is pure, and it enlightens my eyes.

The reverential fear of you is clean, and it endures forever. Your judgments are true and righteous altogether.

More to be desired are they than gold, even the finest gold. They are sweeter than honey and the honeycomb.

By them, O God, I am warned, and in keeping them, I find great reward. Cleanse me from all secret faults.

Keep me, your servant, from all presumptuous sins. Do not ever let them have dominion over me. Then I shall be upright, and I shall be innocent of all transgression.

Let the words of my mouth and the meditation of my heart be acceptable in your sight, O Lord, my strength and my Redeemer.

In the powerful name of Jesus I pray, Amen.

7

Psalm 23 – The Shepherd's Psalm

Thoughts to Ponder Before You Pray: Psalm 23 is known as the Shepherd's Psalm because it utilizes several powerful images to show that the Lord God is our Shepherd.

A good shepherd always meets the needs of his sheep. He takes good care of them by making sure they have adequate food, water, shelter, and protection from all enemies, such as wolves and lions that may seek to devour them. Moreover, a shepherd cares deeply for his sheep, and he leads them to safe pastures of peace and plenty.

In the same ways, our heavenly Father watches out for us, His sheep. He meets all our needs and cares, because He knows how much we need His help, protection, provision, and peace in our lives.

Henry Ward Beecher describes this Psalm as "the sweetest song ever heard."

Prayer: O Lord God, you are my Shepherd, and because this is true, I know I shall never be in want. Thank you for making me lie down in green pastures.

You lead me beside still waters, and you restore my soul. Guide me in the paths of righteousness for your name's sake.

Even though I may walk through the valley of the shadow of death, I will fear no evil, for you are with me. Thank you, Father.

Your rod and your staff bring me great comfort.

Thank you for preparing your table before me in the presence of my enemies. You anoint my head with oil, and my cup overflows.

Surely goodness and mercy will follow me all the days of my life, and I will dwell in your house forever.

In the name of Jesus I pray, Amen.

8

Psalm 24 – The King of Glory

Thoughts to Ponder Before You Pray: Many scholars believe this Psalm may have been written when the Ark of the Covenant was brought to Jerusalem.

Samuel writes, "Now it was told King David, saying, 'The Lord has blessed the house of Obed-Edom and all that belongs to him, because of the ark of God.' So David went and brought up the ark of God from the house of Obed-Edom to the City of David with gladness....Then David danced before the Lord with all his might; and David was wearing a linen ephod. So David and all the house of Israel brought up the ark of the Lord with shouting and with the sound of the trumpet" (2 Sam. 6:12-15, NKJV).

What a triumphant song we find in Psalm 24.

Prayer: Father God, the earth, its fullness, and all who dwell within the world you've created are yours. Thank you for creating this world and for founding it upon the seas and establishing it upon the waters.

Who may ascend to your hill or stand in your holy place? Father, thank you for showing me that those who have a pure heart, have clean hands, have not sworn deceitfully, and have not lifted up their souls to idols will be able to be near to you and receive your blessings and your righteousness.

Help me, Father, to walk in the righteousness you've imparted to me at all times and to be near you always.

Lift up your heads, O you gates; and be lifted up, you everlasting doors, and the King of glory shall come in.

You, Lord God, are the King of glory! You, O God, are strong and mighty in battle. You are the Lord of hosts. You are the King of glory! Thank you for your power, strength, and might in my life.

In the mighty name of Jesus I pray, Amen.

9

Psalm 25 – Guidance and Deliverance

Thoughts to Ponder Before You Pray: In this Psalm of David, we hear the Psalmist's cry for guidance and for deliverance from affliction that has been brought on by his sins. He seeks God's guidance, direction, mercy, forgiveness, and restoration. It is the cry of David's sin-sick soul.

Prayer: Lord God, I lift my soul up to you, and I trust in you. Don't let me be ashamed, and don't let my enemies triumph over me. I thank you for your promise that those who wait on you shall never experience shame.

Show me your ways, O Lord God. Teach me your paths. Lead me in your truth and teach me, for you are the God of my salvation, and I wait on you all day long. Remember, O Lord God, your tender mercies and your lovingkindnesses, for they are from of old.

Do not remember the sins of my youth, nor my transgressions. According to your mercy, remember me, for your goodness' sake, O Lord God.

You are so good and upright, Father, and it is for this reason that you teach sinners in the way. Thank you for guiding and teaching your ways to the humble. Help me to walk in humility, Father.

All of your paths, Lord God, are mercy and truth to those who keep your covenant and your testimonies. I ask for your help, that I will always keep your covenant and your testimonies.

For your name's sake, O Lord God, pardon my iniquity, for it is great. As I reverentially fear and honor you, I ask you to teach me in the way you choose and to enable me to dwell in prosperity. Let my descendants possess their inheritance.

Thank you for showing me that your secret is with those who fear you. Help me to fear and honor you always. Reveal your covenant to me, Father, for my eyes are ever toward you.

Turn yourself to me, and have mercy upon me, I pray, for I am desolate and afflicted. Father, the troubles of my heart have enlarged. Bring me out of my distresses!

Look on my affliction and my pain, and forgive all my sins. Consider my enemies, for they are many, and they hate me with cruel hatred. Keep my soul, and deliver me.

Let me not be ashamed, for I put my trust in you. Let integrity and uprightness preserve me, for I wait for you. Thank you for hearing and answering my prayer.

In Jesus' glorious name I pray, Amen.

10

Psalm 26 – Walking in Integrity

Thoughts to Ponder Before You Pray: Integrity is an unimpaired condition of soundness that derives from ardent adherence to a moral code. It involves soundness of spirit and mind, undivided adherence to God, honesty, and completeness.

Such wonderful integrity is achieved through faith in the completed work of Jesus Christ, who died to free us from our sins and make it possible for us to become righteous in Him.

Paul writes, "I have been crucified with Christ; it is no longer I who live, but Christ lives in me; and the life which I now live in the flesh I live by faith in the Son of God, who loved me and gave Himself for me. I do not set aside the grace of God; for if righteousness comes through the law, then Christ died in vain" (Gal. 2:20-21, NKJV).

Prayer: Vindicate me, O Lord God, for I have walked in the integrity you've imparted to me. Because I have trusted in you, I know I shall not slip. Thank you, Father.

Examine me, and prove me. Try my mind and my heart, for your lovingkindness is before my eyes, as I endeavor to walk in your truth.

I have not sat with idolators, nor will I go with hypocrites. I have hated the assembly of evildoers, and I will not sit with the wicked.

Therefore, I wash my hands in innocence, and I will go about your altar, Lord God. Help me to proclaim your truth with the voice of thanksgiving and tell of all your wondrous works.

Lord God, I love the habitation of your house and the place where your glory dwells. Do not gather my soul with sinners, or my life with bloodthirsty men, in whose hands there are sinister schemes and bribes.

As for me, Father, with your help, I will walk in integrity. O my Redeemer, be merciful to me and make my foot stand in a level place, where I am free from the danger of falling or stumbling. I will ever bless you, Lord God, in the congregation.

In Jesus' wonderful name I pray, Amen.

11

Psalm 27 – Trusting God

Thoughts to Ponder Before You Pray: Trusting God is assured reliance on His character, ability, strength, truth, and love. It involves placing your confidence, faith, and hope in the Father, who is completely trustworthy in every respect.

The author of Proverbs writes: "Trust in the Lord with all your heart, and lean not on your own understanding; in all your ways acknowledge Him, and He shall direct your paths" (Prov. 3:5-6, NKJV).

In Psalm 27, David exhibits fearless trust in God, who is his light, his salvation, and the strength of his life. Let this Psalm become your prayer of commitment and trust, as you express your faith to God.

Prayer: Lord God, you are my light, my salvation, and the strength of my life. Of whom shall I be afraid? Though an army should encamp against me, my heart shall not fear. Though war may rise against me, in this will I be confident.

One thing have I desired of you, Father, and that will I seek — to dwell in your house all the days of my life, to behold your beauty, and to inquire in your temple.

How I praise you, Lord God, for the certain knowledge you have given to me, that you will hide me in your pavilion and in the secret place of your tabernacle in times of trouble and set me high upon a rock.

I claim your promise that my head shall be lifted up above my enemies all around me. Therefore, I offer sacrifices of joy in your tabernacle and I sing praises to you.

Hear me, O Lord God, when I cry with my voice. Have mercy upon me, and answer me. Through your grace, I will seek your face at all times.

My heart's desire is to seek your face. Your face, O God, I will seek.

Do not hide your face from me, Father. Do not turn me away in anger. You have always been my help.

I know you will never leave me nor forsake me, O God of my salvation. Thank you for this precious promise from your Word.

Teach me your way, O Lord God, and lead me in a smooth path, because of my enemies. Deliver me from the will of my adversaries, false witnesses, or any who would do violence against me.

Through faith in you and your Word, Father, I shall not lose heart, because I believe I will see your goodness in the land of the living. Therefore, I wait on you with the good courage you've given to me. Thank you for promising to strengthen my heart as I wait on you.

In Jesus' loving name I pray, Amen.

12

Psalm 31 – Full Confidence in God

Thoughts to Ponder Before You Pray: This Psalm is a wonderful example of David's solid confidence in God. Jesus' dying words came from this Psalm. Luke writes, "And when Jesus had cried out with a loud voice, He said, 'Father, into Your hands I commit My spirit.' Having said this, He breathed His last" (Luke 23:46, NKJV).

Let your faith rise to receive what God has in store for you in the form of protection, guidance, mercy, goodness, and courage, as you pray this Psalm.

Prayer: In you, O Lord God, I put my trust. Never let me be ashamed, and deliver me in your righteousness.

Bow down your ear to me, and deliver me speedily. Be my Rock of refuge, a fortress of defense to save me, for you are my Rock and my fortress. Therefore, for your name's sake, lead me and guide me.

Pull me out of the net, which they have secretly laid for me, for you are my strength. Into your hands I commit my spirit, for you have redeemed me, O Lord God of truth. Thank you for redeeming me. I will have no regard for idols, for all of my trust is in you, Father.

I will be glad and rejoice in your mercy, for you have considered my trouble, you have known my soul in adversities, and you have not shut me up into the hand of the enemy. Thank you for setting my feet in a wide place of freedom from affliction, fear, and harm, dear God.

Have mercy on me, O Lord God, for I am in trouble. I trust in you, Father, for you are my God, and my times are in your hand. Deliver me from the hand of my enemies and from those who persecute me. Make your face to shine upon me, and save me for your mercies' sake.

Do not let me be ashamed, O Lord God, for I have called upon you. Oh, how great is your goodness, which you have laid up for those who fear you, a goodness you have prepared for those who trust you in the presence of others.

Thank you for your promise to hide me in the secret place of your presence. Protect me from the strife of tongues.

Blessed are you, O God, for you have shown me your marvelous kindness in a strong city. You heard the voice of my supplication when I cried out to you. Help me to be of good courage, Father, for I know you are strengthening my heart, as I hope in you.

In the strong and righteous name of Jesus I pray, Amen.

13

Psalm 37 – Do Good, and Don't Worry

Thoughts to Ponder Before You Pray: This Psalm has been greatly loved by believers throughout the centuries, because it reveals the blessings that come to all who trust God, even when wickedness is swirling around them.

Throughout Psalm 37, David vividly contrasts the ways of the wicked with the ways of the righteous. He clearly shows how trusting God, doing good, and ceasing from worry will enable you to reap tremendous benefits both in this life and in the life to come.

As you pray this Psalm, remember that God loves you and always wants the best for you.

Prayer: O God, my Father, help me never to worry because of evil people nor to envy wrong-doers, for I know they will wither like grass.

I choose to trust in you and do good. I will dwell in the land and enjoy safe pasture, and I will delight myself in you. As I do so, I know you will give me the desires of my heart. Thank you, Father.

I commit my way to you, O Lord, and I will trust in you. Thank you for your promise to make your righteousness shine like the dawn and your justice like the noonday.

Help me to rest in you, Father, and to wait patiently for you. In so doing, I will not worry about the wicked who prosper and bring their evil schemes to pass.

Instead, I will cease from anger and forsake all wrath. I will not worry, because it only causes harm to me and others.

Thank you for showing me that evildoers shall be cut off, but those who wait on you will inherit the earth. This enables me to delight myself in the abundance of your peace.

Father, I believe your Word, which assures me that having a little as a righteous person is better than the riches of many wicked. Thank you for upholding the righteous.

Lord God, you know the days of the upright and the inheritance of the upright shall be forever. Thank you, Father.

You promise that the righteous will not be ashamed in the evil time, and in the days of famine they shall be satisfied, but the wicked shall perish.

Your enemies, dear Father, shall perish. Like the splendor of the meadows, they shall vanish. Into smoke, they shall vanish away.

Thank you for showing me that, though the wicked borrows and does not repay, the righteous show mercy and give. Help me always to show mercy and to give freely to those in need.

Father, I realize that the steps of good people are ordered by you and you take delight in the way of the righteous. Therefore, I know that when I fall, I shall not be utterly cast down, for you will uphold me with your hand.

I have been young and now I am older, yet I have never seen the righteous forsaken, nor their descendants begging for bread. Righteous people are ever merciful and they lend to others; their descendants are blessed.

Dear God, I will obey you by departing from evil and doing good. Thank you for your promise that I will dwell securely forever.

You love justice, O Lord, and you will never forsake your people. The righteous will be preserved forever.

Help me, Father, to speak wisdom at all times and to talk of your justice. Your law is in my heart, and none of my steps shall stumble.

I will wait on you, Lord, and keep your way. Thank you for your promise to lift me up.

You, O Lord God, are my strength in all times of trouble. Thank you for your promise to help me and deliver me. I know you will always deliver me from the wicked, because I trust in you.

In the mighty name of Jesus I pray, Amen.

14

Psalm 40 – A Song of Deliverance

Thoughts to Ponder Before You Pray: David knew God as the One who hears and answers prayer. He had experienced God's hand of deliverance in his life on many different occasions. In this Psalm, he praises God for His goodness to him and he expresses his faith and trust to God.

Jesus, also, prayed a portion of this Psalm, as the writer of Hebrews reminds us, "Sacrifice and offering You did not desire. But a body You have prepared for Me. In burnt offerings and sacrifices for sin You had no pleasure. Then I said, 'Behold, I have come — in the volume of the book it is written of Me — to do Your will, O God'" (Heb. 10:5-6, NKJV).

The author of Hebrews explains, "By that will [God's will] we have been sanctified through the offering of the body of Jesus Christ once for all" (Heb. 10:10, NKJV). Be grateful to God for the sanctification He has provided for you through Christ, as you pray this Psalm.

Prayer: Father, I have waited patiently for you, and you have inclined to me and heard my cry. Thank you for bringing me out of a horrible pit of miry clay, setting my feet upon a rock, and establishing my steps.

I praise you for putting a new song in my mouth, a song of praise to you. Let many see these wonderful things you have done in my life, and, in godly fear, place their trust in you, Lord God.

As a result of trusting you, I am filled with happiness. Thank you, Father. You have done so many wonderful things for me. I delight to do your will, O my God, and your law is written within my heart.

Help me to proclaim your good news of righteousness wherever I go. I will not conceal the news of your righteousness within my heart. Instead, I will declare your faithfulness and your salvation to all people.

Do not withhold your tender mercies from me, O God. Let your lovingkindness and your truth continually preserve me. Innumerable evils have surrounded me. My iniquities have overtaken me, so I cannot look up.

Be pleased, O Lord God, to deliver me from all evil and iniquity. Make haste to help me. Deal swiftly with my enemies.

Let all those who seek you rejoice and be glad in you. Thank you, Father, for always being my help and my Deliverer. Do not delay, O my God.

In the glorious name of Jesus I pray, Amen.

15

Psalm 46 – A Mighty Fortress Is Our God

Thoughts to Ponder Before You Pray: The great reformer, Martin Luther, based his triumphant hymn, "A Mighty Fortress Is Our God," on this victorious Psalm. Contemplate Luther's words before you pray:

"A mighty fortress is our God, a bulwark never failing;
Our helper He amid the flood of mortal ills prevailing.
For still our ancient foe doth seek to work us woe
His craft and power are great, and armed with cruel hate,
On earth is not his equal.
"Did we in our own strength confide, our striving would be losing,
Were not the right man on our side, the man of God's own choosing.
Dost ask who that may be? Christ Jesus, it is He —
Lord Sabaoth His name, From age to age the same,
And He must win the battle."

As you pray, remember that Jesus Christ has already won the battle through His death on the cross, and, because this is so, you are more than a conqueror through Him. Paul wrote, "Yet in all these things we are more than conquerors through Him who loved us" (Rom. 8:37, NKJV).

Prayer: Lord God, you are my refuge and my strength. Thank you for being a very present help to me in times of trouble.

Because I know these truths, I will not fear, even if the earth is removed and the mountains are carried into the midst of the sea. I thank you, Father, for the river whose streams make me glad; this river flows from the holy place of your tabernacle. It emanates from your throne in heaven.

Thank you for being with me. In this knowledge, I shall not be moved. Thank you for your wonderful promise to help me, for you, O God, are ever with me, and you are my refuge. Thank you, Father.

I will be still and know that you are my God. It thrills my soul, Father, to know that you will be exalted among the nations throughout the earth. You, O Lord of hosts, are with me, and you will ever be my refuge — my mighty fortress.

In Jesus' name I pray, Amen.

16

Psalm 61 – The Higher Rock

Thoughts to Ponder Before You Pray: In this hymn, which David may have sung while away from home, possibly during the time of Absalom's rebellion, we hear his heart crying for transcendence (the ability to rise above the circumstances of life). In fact, he asks God to lead him to the Rock that is higher than he is.

Jesus and the Word of God are often referred to as the solid rocks upon which we may build our lives safely and securely. All other ground is shifting sand. As you pray, ask God to lead you to the Rock.

Prayer: Hear my cry, O God; attend to my prayer. From the end of the earth I will cry to you when my heart is overwhelmed within me. Lead me to the Rock that is higher than I am.

Thank you for being a shelter for me and a strong tower of protection from the enemy. I will abide in your tabernacle forever, and I will trust in the shelter of your wings, for you, O God, have heard my vows. Thank you for giving me the heritage of those who fear and love your name.

Appoint and release your mercy and truth, your faithfulness and love, to watch over and preserve me. I will sing praise to your name forever, and I will daily perform my vows to you. Thank you, Father, for hearing and answering my prayer.

In the rock-solid name of Jesus I pray, Amen.

17

Psalm 63 – Thirsting for God

Thoughts to Ponder Before You Pray: David composed this hymn while he was in the wilderness. He was fleeing from his son Absalom, but he remained confident in God, that his heavenly Father would take good care of him.

Did you ever go through a wilderness in your own life? Did you feel as if everything around you was parched and dry?

When such spiritual dryness occurs in your life, it is important to remember that God's lovingkindness is better than life. As David did, begin to praise God and bless Him. Remind yourself that God always will satisfy your soul.

Prayer: O God, you are my God. I will seek you early, because my soul thirsts for you, and my flesh longs for you in a dry and thirsty land where there is no water. I have looked for you, Lord God, in the sanctuary, so I could see your power and your glory.

Because your lovingkindness is better than life to me, my lips shall praise you. Thus, I will bless you while I live, and I will lift up my hands in your name. I believe you will satisfy my soul, and my mouth shall praise you with joyful lips.

I will remember you on my bed, Father, and I will meditate upon you through the night, because you have always been my help. Therefore, I rejoice in the shadow of your wings. My soul clings to you, and your right hand holds me up. Thank you, Father.

Deal with my enemies, Lord God, and I shall rejoice in you.

In Jesus' loving name I pray, Amen.

18

Psalm 86 – Teach Me Your Way

Thoughts to Ponder Before You Pray: In this Psalm, David is thanking God for his safe return from captivity. He is asking God to bless his future and to give him His mercy, for he recognizes his need for forgiveness.

The Apostle John tells us, "If we confess our sins, He is faithful and just to forgive us our sins and to cleanse us from all unrighteousness" (1 John 1:9, NKJV).

David knew this truth, also, for he wrote, "For You, Lord, are good, and ready to forgive, and abundant in mercy to all those who call upon you" (Ps. 86:5, NKJV).

Prayer: Bow down your ear, O Lord God, and hear me, for I need you. Preserve my life, for you have made me holy. You are my God. Save me, for I am your servant, and I trust in you.

Be merciful to me, O Lord God, for I cry to you all day long. Give me your joy, as I lift my soul up to you. Thank you for being so good to me. I know you are ready to forgive me, and your abundant mercy is always available to me. Thank you, Father.

Give ear, O Lord God, to my prayer, and attend to the voice of my supplications. In the day of trouble I will call upon you, for I know you will answer me. Thank you, Father.

I thank you for your promise that all nations shall come and worship before you, O Lord God, and they shall glorify you. Hasten that day, Lord God, I pray.

Father, you are very great, and you always do wondrous things. You alone are God.

Teach me your way, Father, and help me to walk in your truth. Unite my heart to fear your name.

I will praise you, O Lord, my God, with all my heart, and I will glorify your name forevermore, for great is your mercy toward me, and you have delivered my soul from death and torment.

You, O Lord God, are full of compassion, gracious, longsuffering, and abundant in mercy and truth. Oh, turn to me and have mercy on me. Give me your strength. Thank you for helping me and comforting me.

In Jesus' glorious name I pray, Amen.

19

Psalm 91 – Promises of Security

Thoughts to Ponder Before You Pray: God is your safe place, your refuge, your strength, your high tower, and your Deliverer. Knowing this, you have no reason to fear.

In this greatly loved Psalm, you learn that God will keep you safe from evil, pestilence, and destruction. He promises to give you angelic protection and to answer your prayers. He promises, also, to be with you and to give you long life.

As you believe these promises, claiming them through prayer, you will receive them. God wants to bless you abundantly.

James writes, "Every good gift and every perfect gift is from above, and comes down from the Father of lights, with whom there is no variation or shadow of turning" (James 1:17, NKJV).

Prayer: Father God, thank you for allowing me to dwell in your secret place and to abide under your shadow. You are my refuge and my fortress; you are my God, and I trust in you.

Thank you for promising to deliver me from the snares of the enemy and from all pestilences. Thank you for covering me with your feathers. I take refuge under your wings, dear Father.

Thank you for your truth, which is my shield and buckler.

Because of the faith your Word imparts to me and the blessings you've promised to me, I will no longer be afraid of any terror, violence, disease, or destruction, for I know you will deal with my enemies and all evil that comes against me. Thank you, Father.

You are my dwelling place, Lord God, and I feel safe and secure in you. Thank you for assuring me that no evil shall befall me, and no plague shall come near my dwelling.

I praise you that you have given your angels charge over me, to keep me in all my ways. Thank you, Father, for the fact that they will bear me up in their hands, lest I would dash my foot against a stone.

I believe your promise, Lord God, that I shall tread upon the lion and the cobra and trample them under foot. Because I have set my love upon you, Father, I know you will deliver me. You will set me on high in your place of protection, because I know your name. I am confident that, as I call upon you, you will answer me, and you will be with me in times of trouble.

Thank you for your promise to deliver me and honor me. I believe and receive your promise that you will satisfy me with long life and show me your salvation.

In the prevailing name of Jesus I pray, Amen.

20

Psalm 92 – A Song of Sabbath Rest

Thoughts to Ponder Before You Pray: The Sabbath is a day of rest for God's people. God promises to give you His rest, as the writer of Hebrews explains, "There remains therefore a rest for the people of God" (Heb. 4:9, NKJV).

In this Psalm, David thanks God for the blessings of rest He gives to His people, and he points to the time when you and all God's people will enjoy the Age of Eternal Sabbath.

Prayer: Father, it is so good to give thanks to you and to sing praises to your name, O Most High. I will declare your lovingkindness every morning and your faithfulness every night. Thank you, Lord God, for making me glad through your works. I will always triumph and take great joy in the works of your hands.

O Lord God, how great are all your works! Your thoughts are very deep. You are on high forevermore, and I thank you for exalting me and making me victorious, and for anointing me with the fresh oil of joy.

I believe and receive your promise that, as one you have made righteous in Christ, I shall flourish like a palm tree and grow like a cedar in Lebanon. Because I have been planted in your house, O Lord, I know I shall flourish in your courts.

Thank you for your promise that I will be fruitful in old age and remain fresh and vigorous. I claim this promise for my life as I pray.

I will always declare that you, Lord God, are upright, and that you are my Rock, and there is no unrighteousness in you.

Thank you, Father, for hearing and answering my prayer.

In the blessed name of Jesus I pray, Amen.

21

Psalm 100 – God's Everlasting Truth and Mercy

Thoughts to Ponder Before You Pray: In this well-known Psalm of thanksgiving, God is honored as your faithful and merciful Creator, and you are encouraged to enter into His gates with thanksgiving and to go into His courts with praise.

As you do so, remember that God is good, His mercy is everlasting, and His truth endures to all generations.

Prayer: Father, I shout joyfully to you, and I serve you with gladness. I come now before your presence with singing, knowing that you are my God. You have created me. I am a sheep in your pasture.

I enter into your gates with thanksgiving, and I come into your courts with praise. As I enjoy your presence, Father, I am thankful to you, and I bless your name, for I know you are good. Thank you for your everlasting mercy and your truth, which endure to all generations.

In the merciful name of Jesus I pray, Amen.

22

Psalm 103 – Bless the Lord!

Thoughts to Ponder Before You Pray: Many scholars believe that David wrote this greatly loved Psalm when he was old. In it, he reflects on God's many benefits to him, including His mercy, His blessings, His faithfulness, and His Word.

In effect, this is a summary of how God dealt so lovingly with David throughout his life. In this Psalm, you will find many promises to claim for your own life.

Prayer: My soul blesses you, Lord God, and all that is within me blesses your most holy name. I will never forget all your benefits to me.

Father, you forgive all my iniquities, heal all my diseases, redeem my life from destruction, crown me with your lovingkindness and tender mercies, satisfy me with so many good things, and renew my youth as the eagle's.

Thank you for executing righteousness and justice for all who are oppressed. I praise you for making your ways known to Moses and performing so many wondrous acts for the children of Israel and for all your children through the ages.

Father, you are merciful and gracious, slow to anger, and abounding in mercy. Thank you for not dealing with me according to my sins and for not punishing me according to my iniquities.

As the heavens are high above the earth, so great is your mercy to me. Thank you for removing my transgressions from me as far as the east is from the west.

Thank you for being my Father and for having compassion on me as a father has compassion on his children. I'm so glad to know, dear God, that you know my frame, and you remember that I am but dust.

Though I realize my life will eventually pass, I know your mercy is from everlasting to everlasting. Thank you, Father. I thank you, also, for promising your mercy to my descendants. Help us always to honor your covenant and give heed to your Word.

Father, you have established your throne in heaven, and your kingdom rules over all. Oh, how I rejoice that your angels, who excel in strength and heed and do your Word, bless you at all times, for they are your ministers who do your pleasure.

I join with all your works in all places of your dominion in blessing you. I bless you, Lord God, with all my soul!

In the blessed name of Jesus I pray, Amen.

23

Psalm 112 – Everlasting Blessedness

Thoughts to Ponder Before You Pray: When your heart is fixed, trusting in and on God, you may justifiably claim His promise to bless you eternally. The prerequisites to this everlasting blessedness, as pointed out by the Psalmist, are fearing God in the sense of reverential awe and delighting greatly in His Word.

The blessings outlined in Psalm 112 include blessings upon your descendants, prosperity, enduring righteousness, light, fearlessness, and the establishment of your heart. This Psalm is truly powerful, and praying this Psalm is purposeful for you.

Prayer: O God, I praise you. Thank you for the promises of blessedness you give to me, as I fear you and greatly delight in your commandments. Help me to fear you and to take great delight in your commandments at all times, dear Father.

I claim your promise that you will fill my home with wealth and riches, and you will cause my righteousness to endure forever. I rejoice that your light has risen in the darkness for me. You are so gracious, Father, full of compassion, and righteous, and I want to be more like you.

Help me to remember to deal graciously with others and to conduct my affairs with discretion. I believe that I shall never be shaken, because of your promises to me.

Father, I will not be afraid of evil tidings, for my heart is steadfast, trusting in you. I will fear, because I know you will deal appropriately with my enemies.

Guide me in giving to the poor and dispersing the blessings you shower upon me. Let my righteousness endure forever, Father, and lift me up in honor, as I give reverence to your name.

Thank you for hearing and answering my prayer, dear God.

In Jesus' righteous name I pray, Amen.

24

Psalm 116 – Answered Prayer

Thoughts to Ponder Before You Pray: The Psalmists experienced answered prayer over and over again. This is a song of gratitude for all those answered prayers, including deliverance from death and temptation.

This beautiful Psalm is filled with God's love, God's grace, and God's mercy. It is a hymn of praise, love, adoration, and thanksgiving to the One who does all things well.

Prayer: Father God, I love you. Thank you for hearing my voice and my supplications. Because you have inclined your ear to me, I will call upon you for as long as I live. Though the pains of death surrounded me, and I found myself in trouble and sorrow, when I called upon you, you delivered me. Thank you, Father.

You are so gracious, righteous, and merciful. Thank you for preserving those who trust you in simple, child-like faith. Your bountiful goodness to me, Father, enables my soul to return to the rest you've provided for me. Thank you, Father.

You have delivered my soul from death, my eyes from tears, and my feet from stumbling. I will walk before you in the land of the living. I believe; therefore, I will ever speak forth your truth. Thank you, Father.

What shall I render unto you for all your benefits to me? I will take up your cup of salvation and call upon your name. I will pay my vows of praise and sing praises to you in the presence of your people.

O Lord God, truly I am your servant. Thank you for loosing my bonds. I will offer to you the sacrifice of thanksgiving, and I will call upon your name.

Praise you, mighty Father. In Jesus' name, Amen.

25

Psalm 119 – The Power
of God's Word

Thoughts to Ponder Before You Pray: This is a vitally important Psalm for you to remember and pray, for it reveals the power of God's Word in your life. In this Psalm and Psalm 19, as well, we discover that "...the word of God is living and powerful, and sharper than any two-edged sword, piercing even to the division of soul and spirit, and of joints and marrow, and is a discerner of the thoughts and intents of the heart" (Heb. 4:12, NKJV).

David wrote, "The law of the Lord is perfect, converting the soul; the testimony of the Lord is sure, making wise the simple; the statutes of the Lord are right, rejoicing the heart; the commandment of the Lord is pure, enlightening the eyes; the fear of the Lord is clean, enduring forever; the judgments of the Lord are true and righteous altogether.

"More to be desired are they than gold, yea, than much fine gold; sweeter also than honey and the honeycomb. Moreover by them Your servant is warned, and in keeping them there is great reward" (Ps. 19:7-11, NKJV).

Psalm 19 serves as a great prelude to the truths packed into Psalm 119. What is the power of God's Word in your life? It brings conversion to your soul and makes you wise. It causes your heart to rejoice and enlightens your eyes. The Word of God is pure, clean, true, righteous, and sweeter than the honeycomb.

It is not surprising, therefore, that Psalm 119 is the longest chapter in the Bible. Almost every verse of this Psalm mentions God's Word. The Psalmist refers to the Word of God as God's law, testimony, judgments, statutes, commandments, precepts, ordinances, ways, and Word.

As you pray this Psalm, remember the importance of God's Word to you, for it is the source of your faith. Paul writes, "So then faith comes by hearing, and hearing by the word of God" (Rom. 10:17, NKJV).

Prayer: Help me to walk in your Word, dear Father. I want to keep your commandments and seek you with my whole heart at all times. Teach me, through your Word, to walk in all your ways.

Help me to keep your precepts diligently, for I know this will keep me from shame. As I look to your Word, Father, praise wells up from deep within me. I will praise you with uprightness of heart and I will keep your statutes. Do not forsake me, dear God.

Thank you for showing me how to cleanse my way by taking heed according to your Word. With my whole heart I seek you, Lord God; don't ever let me wander from your commandments.

Your Word have I hidden in my heart, that I would not sin against you. Blessed are you, dear God. Teach me your statutes. With my lips I will declare all the judgments of your mouth.

I rejoice, mighty God, in the way of your testimonies, far more than I rejoice in all riches. Help me to remember to meditate on your precepts and to contemplate your ways at all times. Father, I will delight myself in your statutes, and I will not forget your Word.

Deal bountifully with me, Lord God, that I may live and keep your Word. Open my eyes, that I may see wondrous things from your law. Remove from me all the reproach and contempt of others, as I endeavor to keep your Word.

Your Word is my meditation all day long, and your testimonies are my delight and my counselors. Revive me according to your Word, dear Father. Teach me your statutes and make me understand the way of your precepts, so I will be able to meditate on all your wonderful works.

Strengthen me according to your Word. Keep me from false and deceitful ways, and graciously guide me by the truth of your Word, for I have chosen the way of truth. I have laid your judgments before me, Father, and I cling to your testimonies.

Thank you for your Word and its truth. I will run in the way of your commandments, Father, for I know you shall enlarge my heart with understanding. Teach me, O Lord God, the way of your statutes, and I shall endeavor to keep them until the end of my life.

Give me understanding, that I may keep your law. Indeed, with your help, I shall observe it with my whole heart. Make me walk in the path of your commandments, Father, for I delight in your Word.

Incline my heart to your testimonies, not to covetousness. Turn my eyes away from looking at worthless things, and give me life in your ways, dear God. Establish your Word in my life, for I am devoted to serving you with reverent fear and worship.

I long for your precepts, Father. In your righteousness, fill me with your life. Let your mercies and steadfast love come to me, even the blessings of your salvation, according to your Word. In this way I shall always have an answer for those who taunt and reproach me, for I trust in your Word.

Do not let your Word of truth ever depart from my mouth, dear God, for I have placed all my hope in your Word. Therefore, I shall keep your Word continually, forever and ever, and will walk in liberty, for I have sought your precepts.

Help me speak of your testimonies before others and never be ashamed. Through your grace, Father, I will delight myself in your commandments, which I greatly love. I will lift up my hands, giving reverence to your commandments which I love, and I will meditate on your statutes continually.

Remember your Word to me, your servant, I pray, for in your Word I have found great hope. This is my comfort, for your Word has given me life. Even though others may hold me in derision at times, I will not turn away from your Word, dear Father.

Because I remember your judgments of old, I have found great comfort. Your words are my songs, Father, wherever I am.

I remember your name in the night, Lord God, and I endeavor always to keep your Word, which has become my personal possession, because you have helped me to keep your precepts.

You are my portion, O Lord God. I have said that I will keep your words, and I mean it. Help me to do that, always. With my whole heart, I ask for your gracious favor to be upon me. Be merciful to me according to your Word.

When I thought on my own ways, I turned my feet in the direction of your testimonies. I made haste and did not delay in keeping your commandments. Even though the cords of the wicked have sometimes ensnared me, I have always remembered your Word.

At midnight I will rise to thank you, Father, for your Word, your righteous judgments, and your goodness to me. I am a companion and friend of all who reverence you, as I do, and of those who keep your precepts. The earth, O Lord God, is full of your mercy. Teach me your statutes.

Thank you for dealing so well with me, your servant, according to your Word. Teach me good judgment and knowledge, for I believe your Word. In past days, dear God, I wandered away, but now I keep your Word. Help me, Father.

You are good, and you do good. Please teach me your statutes. Even when the proud lie about me, I will keep your precepts with my whole heart, because I delight in your Word, dear Father.

Thank you for your dealings in my life. They have helped me learn the power of your Word and the importance of keeping your statutes. Your Word, dear God, is better to me than great riches.

Your hands have made and fashioned me, dear Father. Give me understanding, that I may learn the truth of your Word. Those who reverence and honor you will be glad when they see me, because they will know I have hoped in your Word. Thank you, Father.

Thank you for your mercy and faithfulness in my life. Let your merciful kindness be for my comfort, Father. Let your tender mercies come to me, that I may live, for your Word is my delight. Deal with the proud, Father, and help me to remember to meditate on all your precepts.

Let my heart be blameless and sincere as I regard your statues, that I may not be ashamed. I find my hope in your Word, Father. All your commandments are faithful. Fill me with your life, according to your lovingkindness, that I may keep the testimonies of your mouth.

O Lord God, I thank you that your Word is settled forever in heaven and your faithfulness endures to all generations. You established the earth, and it abides. Unless your Word had been my delight, I would have perished in my affliction.

I will never forget your precepts, for by them you have given me life. Thank you, Father, that I am yours. Help me, for I follow after your precepts. I will always give consideration to your testimonies and remember that your commandments are a boundless source of wisdom for me.

Oh, how I love your Word, dear God! It is my meditation all the day. Through your commandments, I receive wisdom, for your words are ever with me.

Your testimonies are my meditation, and I desire to keep your precepts. Help me, Father, to restrain my feet from every evil way, so I would always keep your Word.

Guide me in the paths of your truth, for you are my teacher and guide. Keep me from ever departing from your judgments, for you have taught me. How sweet are your words to my taste. Father, they are sweeter to me than honey.

Through your precepts, I gain understanding; therefore, I hate every false way. Thank you for your Word, Father.

Your Word is a lamp unto my feet and a light to my path. Help me to walk in the light of your Word each step of the way, Father.

I am committed to keeping your righteous judgments. Fill me with your life, O Lord God, according to your Word.

Accept, I pray, the freewill offerings of my mouth, Father God, and teach me your truths. Help me always to remember your Word.

I have taken your testimonies as a heritage forever from your hands, Father. Thank you so much for the inheritance I have found in your Word. Truly, it is the rejoicing of my heart.

Help me to be sure that my heart is inclined to perform your statutes to the very end, Father. I hate double-mindedness, but I love your law.

You are my hiding place and my shield, and I hope in your Word. Thank you, Father.

Uphold me according to your Word, dear God, that I may live, and never let me be ashamed of my hope in you and your wonderful Word.

Hold me up, and I shall be safe and continually observe your statutes. Thank you, Father.

Deal with me according to your mercy and steadfast love, and teach me your statutes, for I am your servant. Give me understanding, that I may know your testimonies.

I love your commandments far more than gold. Thank you for your Word. All its precepts are right, and they lead me to hate every false way.

Your testimonies are wonderful, dear God. Therefore, my soul desires to keep them at all times.

The entrance of your words gives light and brings understanding to me. Look upon me, and be merciful to me, as you are to all those who love your name.

Direct my steps by your Word, dear Father, and don't let iniquity have dominion over me. Redeem me from the oppression of others, that I may keep your precepts.

Make your face shine upon me, and teach me your statutes. I weep, Father, when I see others failing to honor your Word. Reveal your truth to them.

You are righteous, Lord God, and your judgments are upright. Your testimonies are righteous and very faithful. Your Word is very pure, and I greatly love it.

Lord God, your righteousness is an everlasting righteousness, and your law is truth. Your commandments are my delight. The righteousness of your testimonies is everlasting. Give me understanding that I may live.

I cry out with my whole heart, Father, asking you to hear me and to help me keep your statutes. I hope in your Word.

Through the night, I will meditate on your Word. Hear my voice according to your lovingkindness, and give me life according to your justice.

Thank you for being near to me, Father, and for the truth of all your commandments. Great are your tender mercies, dear God; revive me according to your judgments.

Consider how I love your precepts, and fill me with your life, according to your lovingkindnesses.

The entirety of your Word, O God, is truth, and every one of your righteous judgments endures forever. My heart stands in awe of your Word.

I rejoice in your Word, as one who has found a great treasure. I hate and abhor lying, Father, but I love your Word.

I have great peace because I love your Word, and nothing can make me stumble. Lord God, I hope for your saving protection as I obey your Word.

Help me to keep your testimonies, for I love them exceedingly. It is my desire to keep your precepts and your testimonies, for all my ways are known before you.

Let my cry come before you, O Lord God. Give me understanding according to your Word.

Let my supplication come before you, and deliver me according to your Word. My lips shall praise you, for you are teaching me your statutes. Thank you, Father.

My tongue shall speak of your Word, for all your commandments are righteousness. Let your hand help me, for I have chosen your precepts.

Your law is my delight, dear Father. Because my soul lives, I shall praise you. Let your judgments help me.

Thank you for hearing and answering my prayer, dear God, and thank you for the power of your Word in my life. I am committed to you and your Word forever.

In Jesus' mighty name I pray, Amen.

26

Psalm 121 – The Lord Will Keep You

Thoughts to Ponder Before You Pray: This beloved Psalm points the reader to God, who is the source of help for every believer. It contains many special promises for you to claim for your own life.

Prayer: I lift up my eyes to the hills, to you, O God, unto your glorious majesty. I thank you for being my source of help at all times. You are my Creator, and you have made heaven and earth. All my help comes from you.

Thank you for your promise that you will not allow my foot to be moved, and you will never slumber nor sleep. You are my Keeper, Lord God. You protect me and watch over me.

Thank you for being the shade at my right hand, and for your promise to preserve me from all evil. Father, I claim these promises for my life right now.

Keep me from all evil, Lord God, and preserve my soul. Guard and protect my going out and my coming in from this time forth and forevermore.

Thank you for hearing and answering my prayer. In Jesus' name I pray, Amen.

27

Psalm 138 – God Hears and Answers Prayer

Thoughts to Ponder Before You Pray: This Psalm of David emphasizes many important truths about God. Foremost, you should praise Him for His lovingkindness and His truth.

God has magnified His Word and His name above all things. He hears and answers prayer. In response to your prayers, He will give you strength, revive you, save you from all enemies, and perfect that which concerns you.

These facts of your faith will make you want to praise and worship God with all your heart.

Prayer: O God, I will praise you with my whole heart. I will sing praise unto you, and I will worship toward your holy temple. I praise your name for your lovingkindness and your truth, for you have magnified your Word and your name above all things.

In the day when I cried out, you answered me and made me bold with strength in my soul. Thank you, Father.

Your glory is so great, dear God. Though you are on high, you give regard to the lowly. Thank you for giving regard to me.

Though I walk in the midst of trouble, I know you will preserve me and keep me alive. Thank you that you stretch out your hand against the wrath of my enemies and your right hand will save me.

Thank you for promising to perfect that which concerns me, O Father. I know your mercy endures forever. Thank you for your promise that you will never leave me nor forsake me.

In Jesus' precious name I pray, Amen.

28

Psalm 141 – Protection From Sin

Thoughts to Ponder Before You Pray: David, in this Psalm, seeks God's protection from sin. He asks God to set a guard over his mouth and a watch over his lips.

It is clear that David did not want to be enticed into sin of any kind, and this is a great example for each believer to follow.

Prayer: Father God, I cry out to you. Make haste to help me. Give ear to my voice when I cry out to you, and let my prayer be as incense before you. Let the lifting of my hands in prayer be as the evening sacrifice.

Set a guard, O Lord God, over my mouth, and keep watch over the door of my lips. Help me not to incline my heart to any evil thing, for I never want to practice wickedness in any form, nor do I ever want to partake of evil delicacies.

Through your grace, Father, if a righteous person corrects me, I shall receive it as a kindness. If a righteous person rebukes me, Father, I will receive it as excellent oil. Keep me from ever refusing such correction and rebukes, Lord God. Help me to honor you at all times.

My prayer is against the deeds of the wicked. Deal with them, Father. My eyes are ever upon you, O Lord, my God. In you I take refuge.

Keep my soul safe, and protect me from the snares laid for me by evildoers and from the traps of the workers of iniquity. Deliver me from all snares the evil one places in my way.

Let the wicked fall into their nets, while I safely escape. Thank you for hearing and answering my prayer, dear God.

In the righteous name of Jesus I pray, Amen.

Psalm 145 – Praise the Lord!

Thoughts to Ponder Before You Pray: It is fitting for the Psalms to conclude with so many songs of praise. Psalms 135-139 are hymns of thanksgiving, and Psalms 144-150 are songs of praise.

These Psalms are careful to praise God for His wonderful works, miracles, mercy, answers to prayer, universal presence, infinite knowledge, victory, power, faithfulness, and goodness.

The following prayer sets a good standard for you to use as you honor God through praise and thanksgiving.

Prayer: I extol you with high praises, my God and King! I will bless your name forever.

Every day I will praise you, and I will bless your name forever. O my God, you are so great and greatly to be praised. Truly, your greatness is unsearchable.

Let all generations praise your works and declare your mighty acts. As for me, I will speak of your glorious honor and majesty, and I will declare all your wondrous works. Indeed, I will proclaim your greatness, O God.

I will tell of your great goodness, and I will sing of your righteousness, for you, dear

Father, are gracious, full of compassion, slow to anger, and great in mercy.

Thank you for being good to all, dear God. Your tender mercies are over all you have made. All your works shall praise you, and your saints will bless you.

Your people will speak of the glory of your kingdom, and they will talk of your power. In these ways, they will make your mighty acts and the glorious majesty of your kingdom known to all.

Father, your kingdom is an everlasting kingdom, and your dominion endures throughout all generations. You uphold all who fall, and you raise up those who are bowed down.

The eyes of your people wait expectantly upon you, and you give them their food in due season. You open your hand and satisfy the desire of every living thing.

I praise you, Lord God, for you are righteous in all your ways, and gracious in all your works. Thank you for always being near to those who call upon you, to those who call upon you in truth.

I rejoice in your goodness, Father, for you always fulfill the desires of those that reverentially fear you. You hear their cry, and you will save them.

Thank you for preserving all who love you. My mouth will speak your praises. Let all flesh bless your holy name for ever and ever.

Praise you, O Lord God! Hallelujah!

In the blessed name of Jesus I pray, Amen.

Prayers

of

the

Psalmists

Many of the Psalms are written in the form of personal prayers. This enables you to use them freely in your own personal prayer life and devotions, as if you were praying them for yourself.

In this chapter, we use only Psalms that were originally formatted as prayers. In some cases, we have employed only relevant portions of the particular Psalm under consideration. In every case, we have taken the liberty of personalizing each prayer and adapting the Psalms in such a way as to make them effective prayers based on God's Word.

We have based the personalizing of these prayers on the King James Version of the Bible, because it lends itself so well to prayer and devotional reading. Each prayer is an adaptation and paraphrase of the original.

We have given each one a title that addresses the central theme of the particular Psalm being used. These prayers are arranged according to the order in which they appear in the Psalter.

As you read and reflect on these Psalms, you may wish to turn them into prayers for your own life or the lives of others. In so doing, you will see how the prayers of the Psalmists express many of the cries of your heart.

(Please note: In this chapter we've selected only some of the Psalms that were originally transcribed as prayers. In other chapters, you will find additional Psalms that adapt themselves readily to your own prayer life.)

1

A Prayer of Trust (Psalm 3)

Author: David, written after he fled from Absalom, his third son. (Read 2 Sam. 15.) In spite of his son's rebellion, David trusted in God, and this enabled him to rest and sleep peacefully.

Prayer: Lord God, help me when people rise up to trouble me and come against me. Sustain me when people try to tell me that there is no help for me in you.

Help me ever to remember that you, O Lord God, are a shield for me — my glory, and the lifter of my head. I love you, Father, and I know you love me. Thank you for your love.

I cry unto you with my voice, and I know you hear me from your holy hill. I will lie down and sleep, knowing that, when I awake, you, O Lord God, will have sustained me.

Therefore, I will not be afraid though many people may set themselves against me. Indeed, I will not fear, for I know you are with me, and I trust in you with all my heart. Thank you for removing all fear from me, Father, as I place my full trust in you.

Arise, O Lord God. Save me, O my God. Thank you for dealing with all my enemies. I praise you for fighting this battle with me and for me.

Salvation belongs unto you, O Lord God, and your blessing is upon me and all your children. Thank you for all the blessings I enjoy. Selah.

In Jesus' name I pray, Amen.

(Adapted and paraphrased from Psalm 3.)

(Note: The word "Selah," which is used in the preceding Psalm and many others, is a Hebrew word that was used to show a type of interlude in the musical accompaniment to a song. It may well have been a musical direction calling for the clashing of cymbals in order to emphasize a dramatic action God took in the Psalmist's behalf.)

2

A Bedtime Prayer (Psalm 4)

Author: David, who is preparing to go to sleep in the midst of troubling times. He expresses great faith, trust, and confidence in God.

Prayer: Hear me when I call, O God of my righteousness. Thank you for always providing me with relief whenever I have been in distress. The peace you've given to me fills me with a strong sense of security, Father.

Have mercy upon me, and hear my prayer. Thank you for putting gladness in my heart. I am so glad and joyful in you, Father.

I will lie down in peace now and sleep, for you alone, O Lord God, make me to dwell in safety. Thank you for the safety and security I have in you.

The peace you've imparted to me helps me experience your rest at all times. Thank you, Father.

I praise you for hearing and answering my prayer. In Jesus' precious name I pray, Amen.

(Adapted and paraphrased from Psalm 4.)

3

A Morning Prayer (Psalm 5)

Author: David, who, in spite of being pursued by many enemies, shouts for joy, because he knows God will help him and protect him.

Prayer: Give ear to my words, O Lord God, and consider my meditation. Hearken unto the voice of my cry, my King and my God, as I pray unto you.

I know you hear my voice this morning, dear Father, as I direct my prayer to you. I look up to you, for you are not a God who takes pleasure in wickedness, and no evil shall dwell with you. Thank you, Father.

As for me, I come now into your presence, fully aware of the multitude of your mercies in my life. With reverential awe, I worship you. Thank you for your abundant mercies in my life.

Lead me, O Lord God, in your righteousness. Make your way straight before my face. I rejoice as I place my trust in you.

Help me to trust you more and more, and let me ever shout for joy, because I know you will always defend me. I love your name, Father, and I am joyful in you.

Thank you, O Lord God, for your promise to bless the righteous. Help me to walk always in your righteousness. As I do so, I know your favor will surround me as a shield.

In Jesus' righteous name I pray, Amen.

(Adapted and paraphrased from Psalm 5.)

4

A Prayer of Repentance (Psalm 6)

Author: David, in shame and remorse over sin, perhaps his sin with Bathsheba. It was also a time of sickness in David's life.

Prayer: O Lord God, do not rebuke me in anger nor chasten me with your hot displeasure. Have mercy upon me, Father, for I am weak. Heal me, for my bones are troubled. My soul is also greatly troubled.

O Lord God, deliver my soul. Forgive me for your mercies' sake. I am so weary with my groaning. All night long I drench my bed with tears.

I seek your forgiveness, Father, and I ask you to forgive me and cleanse me from all unrighteousness, as I repent of all my sins. [Take time now to confess specific sins to your heavenly Father.] Thank you for forgiving, healing, and cleansing me.

You, Lord God, have heard my supplication, and I thank you for hearing and answering my prayer.

In Jesus' perfect name I pray, Amen.

(Adapted and paraphrased from Psalm 6.)

5

A Prayer for Protection (Psalm 7)

Author: David, at a time when he was being pursued by one of Saul's officers, possibly a man named Cush, the Benjamite.

Prayer: O Lord, my God, in you do I put my trust. Save me from all who persecute me. Deliver me, and protect me I pray.

O Lord, my God, if there is any iniquity in my hands, if I have repaid evil to one who was at peace with me, or have sinned against others in any way, show me how I can make it right with them, and forgive me of my sins.

Arise, O Lord God. Lift yourself up and deal with my enemies, as only you can do. Rise up for me, and fulfill the judgment you have commanded. Let the congregation of your people gather around you.

Father, I ask you to minister to me from on high. Protect me, and help me to walk in your righteousness and integrity at all times.

Let the wickedness of the wicked come to an end, but establish the just. Thank you for being completely righteous, O God, and for testing the hearts and minds of all people, including me. Establish me in your justice, O God.

My defense is of you, Father, because I know you always save the upright in heart. I will praise you according to your righteousness, and I will sing praises to your name, O Most High.

Thank you for hearing and answering my prayer. In the holy name of Jesus I pray, Amen.

(Adapted and paraphrased from Psalm 7.)

6

A Prayer of Adoration (Psalm 8)

Author: David sings this Psalm while reflecting on the Messiah's triumphant reign and the authority we have in Him over all God's creation.

Prayer: O Lord my God, how excellent is your name in all the earth! Your glory is set above the heavens. Out of the mouth of babes and nursing infants you have ordained strength, that you would still the enemy and the avenger. Thank you, Father, for stilling the enemy and the avenger in my life.

When I consider the heavens, the work of your fingers, the moon and the stars, which you have ordained, I wonder what is man, that you are mindful of him, and the son of man, that you visit him?

You have made him a little lower than the angels, and you have crowned him with glory and honor. You made him to have dominion over the works of your hands, and you have put all things under his feet, including sheep, oxen, beasts of the field, birds, fish, and every creature that lives in the sea.

O Lord God, how excellent is your name in all the earth! Thank you for the dominion and authority I have in Christ, my Savior.

In the powerful name of Jesus I pray, Amen.

(Adapted and paraphrased from Psalm 8.)